What the media said about N
Notes from an even Small

"He pokes fun at Singaporeans... but rather than bristle at his observations, you are likely to twitch with mirth. The ribbing is always cushioned by good-natured quips often sprinkled with hilarious anecdotes." — *The Sunday Times*

"The book presents a warts-and-all view of the city-state and celebrates many of the things most often criticised." — *BBC World*

"A candid look at the idiosyncrasies of Singapore and Singaporeans." — *TODAY*

"It's a great insider's look at Singapore from an outsider's point of view." — Malaysia's *Sunday Mail*

"Humphreys' laugh-a-minute self-deprecating manner makes this book very entertaining... No punches pulled. Bravo!" — Malaysia's *Sunday Star*

"Humphreys' humourous take on Singapore is an entertaining read... It is hard not to smile while reading this book." — *Woman's World*

"Blatant prejudices are chewed on, digested and spat out with an equal measure of candour and tongue-in-cheek." — *Singapore Seventeen*

"A thoroughly enjoyable read on the virtues (or hazards) of living in Singapore through the eyes of a 6-foot-4-inch Briton whose style is so disarmingly honest, you will laugh at the things you once considered the bane of your existence... Decidedly Singaporean, distinctly British." — *Singapore FHM*

Scribbles
from the
Same Island

Neil Humphreys

TIMES EDITIONS

Cover picture by Cedric Lim

© 2003 Times Media Private Limited
Published by Times Editions
An imprint of Times Media Private Limited
A member of Times International Publishing
Times Centre, No 1 New Industrial Road
Singapore 536196
Tel (65) 6213 9288 Fax (65) 6285 4871
Email: te@tpl.com.sg
Online bookstore: http://www.timesone.com.sg/te

Times Subang
Lot 46, Subang Hi-Tech Industrial Park
Batu Tiga, 40000 Shah Alam
Selangor Darul Ehsan, Malaysia
Tel & Fax (603) 5636 3517
Email: cchong@tpg.com.my

National Library Board (Singapore)
Cataloguing in Publication Data
Humphreys, Neil (Neil John), 1974–
Scribbles from the Same Island /
Neil Humphreys. – Singapore : Times Editions, c2003.
p. cm.
ISBN : 981-232-589-1
1. Singapore – Anecdotes. I. Title.
DS609   959.57 — dc21   SLS2003014126

Printed in Singapore by Utopia Press Pte Ltd

CONTENTS

ACKNOWLEDGEMENTS

THERE are many kind people I'd like to blame for forcing me to write a second book. P N Balji, my big boss at *TODAY*, was convinced that the newspaper's readers would be interested in my meandering drivel. I must thank him and everyone at *TODAY* who said: "Produce a witty column every Saturday or you're sacked."

The persistence of Times Media, my publisher, should also be acknowledged. After the unexpected success of my first book, there was a polite enquiry about a sequel. Within six months, this had given way to: "Give us another book, you lazy bastard."

I'm grateful, too, for my family's generosity. I've nicked just about every funny story they've ever told me and I've yet to be sued by either my inspirational mother, my sister, Jodie, or any of the Garys that I know.

As always, the missus is on hand to say: "I don't know why you bother, your writing's still crap." Thanks, Tracy, for tolerating all that late-night typing.

But the nights were spent in the incomparable world of Toa Payoh, where the residents are funny, warm, honest and occasionally insane. It's the greatest community I've ever known. Thank you, Toa Payoh, for putting up with this *ang moh*.

INTRODUCTION

I CAN'T stand expatriate columns in Asian newspapers. They are, invariably, full of condescending crap. You either get the '10 Best Pubs in Singapore' rubbish or the paternalistic CEO who is down with local culture because he eats chicken rice and has visited a hawker centre twice.

So when my bosses at *TODAY* toyed with the idea of me writing a weekly 'expat column', I lied and said I was keen. But I really wasn't interested. Who would I be writing for? What would I say? I don't know many of the white community in Singapore. We have little in common. So I kept stalling.

Of course, I could see P N Balji's frustration. My big boss was launching *WEEKEND TODAY*, a new edition of the paper for weekend readers, and wanted the content to be a little off the beaten track. At the same time, my first book on Singapore — *Notes from an even Smaller Island* — had sold remarkably well and was still on the best-seller list when *WEEKEND TODAY* was launched.

But I sincerely believed that I'd said all I had to say about Singapore in my first book. As much as I'd like to, I can't forever stress the need for landladies to walk around with their boobs out. Being the eternal pessimist, I wasn't even sure my style was suitable for a national newspaper.

Then, a magazine asked me to write a one-off piece and it all went a bit bloody crazy. The deal was, the book would get a plug in return for an article on Sarong Party Girls. You know, those Singaporean women who supposedly go for white men with big wallets. Here we go again, I thought. There's me fighting to avoid writing a weekly column full of Western stereotypes and they're asking me to comment upon possibly the biggest. So I reached a compromise. I would only do it, if I could move away from the SPG thing and talk more about inter-racial relationships in Singapore. They agreed.

And my bosses at *TODAY* hit the roof. I wasn't in the meetings, but I think the gist of the discussion was: "This *ang moh* prima donna won't write for us, but the bastard does for everybody else! Get this article in *WEEKEND TODAY*."

When I explained that this wasn't an expat column, just me rambling on about both the British and Singaporean cultures, S Murali, the *WEEKEND TODAY* editor, replied: "That's all we want. Just write in the same way you wrote your book, whenever you have an issue. And make sure it's bloody funny."

Two weeks later, the article was being discussed everywhere. In offices, coffee shops and on national radio. I was being praised by around 80 per cent of the emails I received and threatened by social, and literal, castration by the other 20. I even received email requests from troubled readers who wanted 'agony aunt' advice about their inter-racial relationships. It was an astonishing public reaction. Subsequently, "whenever you have an issue" became "Every bloody week and we don't care if you're trapped in freezing conditions in the Arctic and have lost the use of your hands." So when the publisher asked me to get off my arse and write a second book on Singapore, I thought of the columns in *WEEKEND TODAY*.

Wait, don't put this book back on the shelf. I haven't just lazily thrown together a dozen columns and said 'buy this'. There are completely new topics in here that just couldn't be discussed in a family newspaper. Moreover, I often spend more time cutting my columns than I actually do writing them. So I liked the possibility of expanding and updating them and, of course, using more colourful language. It's not me, you understand, but I must be accurate when putting words in my mother's mouth. She criticised the first book for it's lack of authenticity. She never swore enough.

So here is the second book on Singapore that I never intended to write. If you bought the first book and/or read my columns in *WEEKEND TODAY*, then it's all your bloody fault.

Neil Humphreys
May 2003

THE SPG

FOR some reason, I am an endless source of fascination for taxi drivers in Singapore. After being told I'm from London, they always ask: "So, your wife Singaporean?"

"No, I'm not married. Sorry." (First shock)

"Oh, you stay here? Trellis Towers?"

"No, the HDB block opposite, in Toa Payoh." (Second shock)

"Oh, your girlfriend Singaporean?"

"No, she's British too." (Third shock).

Yes, I'm sorry to disappoint, but my long-time girlfriend, Tracy, is of the English working-class variety and I was with her before I came to Singapura, that sunny island in the sea.

"What, girlfriend *ang moh* ah? Then why you come to Singapore, ah?"

Let's face it, you can hardly blame the average taxi driver. We all know what he's talking about. I come from London — that fab and groovy place with democracy, a two-party political system and pornography. Why else would a single white male leave all that for Singapore, if not for the chance to pocket a fat enough paycheck so he can live in a nice condo, invite tanned, bikini-clad Singaporean girls over for pool parties, and sample the local flavours, so to speak?

To quote my eloquent Singaporean colleague on the Sports Desk: "Don't bluff ah. You bastards come over here, take our money, bang our women, and then leave."

He's only joking of course, but the sad truth is: If there weren't expats over here doing that, then his joke would have no meaning and it wouldn't be funny.

It hasn't happened to me though God knows I've tried. I haven't really. I'm quite happy with my missus — besides she'd cut the old balls off if I did, and deservedly so. I've heard of stories where Westerners have come over with their wives but have still felt compelled to have a taste of the local cuisine.

Though the *ang mohs* are wankers for cheating on their wives, they shouldn't be apportioned all the blame. Despite the recession, the predators are certainly out there, sniffing for good looks, fat wallets and condos (I have none of them so I'm pretty safe).

In fact, living in an HDB flat, I've certainly caught the attention of the ladies around Toa Payoh. But they've caught me first thing in the morning, unshaved and wearing unwashed clothes, sleepily buying bread at the mini-mart. Hardly Brad Pitt, more like a gravel pit.

But I have seen the *ang moh* hunters in action, with my very own eyes, dozens of times in my seven years here. I've seen so many Singaporean women approaching white guys at a bar to start a conversation. It's even happened to me once at Zouk.

Because I'm an ugly bugger and it was dark, the two young ladies said they found me funny. Unfortunately, I wasn't cracking any jokes at that time, but merely trying to dance to garage music.

In my first job here as a teacher, I had a Canadian colleague who deliberately went looking for young, Caucasian-favouring Singaporean ladies mostly at Papa Joe's — that old *ang moh* haven along Orchard Road — a place he described as having "an impressive strike rate".

I remember one of his Chinese girlfriends, in her mid-20s, who told me she had only ever dated white men. Slightly stunned, I asked her why, and she said that Singaporean men were "so boring, childish and predictable" (her words, not mine).

Personally, I feel that her judgement is a little unfair — tedious arseholes are a universal phenomenon. Men who really find a new handphone and all its ringtones exciting, think it's super cool to work 14 hours a day, and find talk of property prices, stocks and shares and Tiger Woods riveting, exist from here to Zaire. Though I must confess I've stumbled into more than my fair share of these boring sods in Singapore. But if I'm being honest here, you only have to look beyond their wallets and their company cars and there are plenty of *ang mohs* in the boring category too.

Yet, despite that, I have noticed what I'll call the "Western-educated Asian" phenomenon. Singaporean women who went to universities in the West, particularly Britain, tend to gravitate more to Western men when they return.

After all, they now "get" Ali G's jokes, follow the trials and tribulations of Cherie Blair and know what Damon Albarn in Blur is singing about in his ditties about suburban life in Britain.

You don't see it the other way round very often, do you? A gang of Chinese blokes, educated in, say, Manchester or Sheffield, hanging out at Boat Quay with a group of blonde bombshells who have big fat purses is a sight I've yet to see.

To be honest, I'd happily give up a week's salary to watch that. But, I'm deeply disappointed to admit that I've often been a major letdown to the Western wannabe. While some of them think they've got lots in common with me, I must admit, the feeling isn't that mutual.

Firstly, Westerners are just so much better at being Western — and that's one of the reasons I left in the first place. If I wanted to get pissed in pubs, fall over and then vomit on the road, I could have stayed in London. The beer is cheaper, more plentiful and tastes better. I didn't come halfway round the world to do that down at Emerald Hill. Secondly, my England, if you like, is vastly different from the England of the average Singaporean overseas student.

On a couple of occasions, I've nodded politely when a beautiful young Singaporean girl waxes lyrical about Yorkminster or the Roman relics of Bath. And she has usually dragged me to a Delifrance or some other overpriced Eurocentric café to do it, too.

Ms. Delifrance often feels she cannot find the same "intellectual" or "soulful" connection with some poor sod who grew up in the HDB heartlands. This is a double irony, of course, because not only is there a statistically high chance that she actually grew up in an HDB block herself, but I also grew up in the London equivalent of a three-room flat.

So what I really want to say is: "Look, I grew up in a working-class council housing estate in Dagenham, which is just outside of East London. I never had the money to go to Yorkminster or Bath, and I had never even been in a pretentious Delifrance until 20 minutes ago, when you invited me. Now, are you going to eat the rest of that overpriced curry puff, or not?"

But a Sarong Party Girl, who supposedly favours all things white and rich, is different. I usually meet them through that aforementioned Canadian colleague of mine, and for those girls (at least, the ones I managed to have conversations with; some were one-night stands I never got to meet), it was a case of money, casual sex, a brief fling or, occasionally, a bit of all three.

The best part was, the Canadian cad never actually had any money and often relied on his British credit card (me). But I believe — and I know I'm going to get a custard pie in my face for this one — money is the ultimate goal. Can we just be honest here for a minute? Whenever we've walked down Orchard Road and observed inter-racial relationships where one of the partners is Caucasian, how many toilet cleaners or garbage collectors make up the numbers?

Do you ever hear a beautiful young Singaporean say: "Have you met Graham? He's from England. We first met when he was flushing out the u-bend of the toilets at my apartment. He just has a wonderful smell about him, don't you think?"

It just doesn't happen like that. Aside from money, there is undoubtedly an element of social climbing involved. Having watched a couple of Singaporean girl-Western man relationships, I've noticed that the girls from the HDB heartlands often begin to act like they were educated at Eton. And where the hell did that accent come from?

A former colleague of my girlfriend was an avowed SPG. She was pleasant company until she met up with Mr. Prat (not his real name). He is one of those upper middle-class Brits, who's always very pleased with himself and is convinced that every utterance he makes is jaw-droppingly funny (a complete prick, in other words.) For some reason, Singapore has had to endure more than its fair share of these boring Brits, especially around the Padang area at City Hall.

Yet, our friend hung on Prat's every word and even attempted to ape his plummy Hugh Grant accent, which was hilarious, because she would flit from Emma Thompson to Liang Po Po in a single sentence. For example, one day over lunch, she told me that Prat's hair was ginger, only she pronounced it with two 'Gs' (as in got or go). I nearly choked on my sesame chicken.

She now wears clothes where the labels are actually genuine and not pasted on by the uncle at the *pasar malam* (night market) — and Prat has a stunningly attractive woman on his arm who pretends to find his jokes funny. Do they love each other and is there a future in the relationship? I have no idea. It is never easy to mesh cross-cultural values together anywhere in the world.

I know the traditional Asian value of filial piety will be a stumbling block eventually, because Ms. Papa Joe's has elderly parents here and yet both she and Prat want to live in the English countryside (naturally) — so something has got to give.

Prat also finds it extremely difficult to have sex with his partner when he knows her parents are asleep in the next room. After all, they are not 18 anymore. But he always seems to get the job done, nonetheless.

As for me, I personally hope that genuine Singaporean girls want more out of a relationship than just regular sex, an affected, artificial accent and Prada bags.

If they don't and they're really that empty, then they might as well rip up the Women's Charter and follow Prat back to the caves, where they can sit around and laugh at "oh-so-Western-aren't-we-intellectual" type jokes.

To be honest, I'd rather have a meaningful relationship with a taxi driver than an SPG. It'd be more stimulating and my girlfriend wouldn't cut my testicles off for it.

NEIL'S NOTE: I was actually asked to write this article by a women's magazine. Initially, I was most reluctant to touch on the subject of SPGs because it was such a cliché. My first book avoided the topic, quite deliberately, almost completely. So I agreed to write the piece, only on condition that I could go beyond the tanned legs and the sarong jokes to talk about this discernible obsession in some quarters with all things Western, which, quite frankly, gets on my bloody nerves. But the magazine article caused quite a stir, so my editor reproduced it in *TODAY* and it all got a little bit surreal after that. For a couple of weeks, I became one of Singapore's most loathed/loved men all at once. Despite the ongoing water disputes with Malaysia at that time, it became one of the most popular discussion topics in the country. Unsurprisingly, Singaporean men praised it and those in inter-racial relationships, er, didn't! But over 80 per cent of the responses were complimentary, rather than critical.

And somehow, it gave birth to a weekly column. But some of the replies I received, well!

THE REPLIES

WELL, I have ruffled a few feathers, haven't I? My relatively harmless topic of superficial, inter-racial relationships has generated the sort of response usually reserved for greedy bus operators who extort an extra five cents from their customers.

The newspaper that I work for, *TODAY*, received more letters about SPGs, Western wannabes and Caucasians living in Singapore than it did on the government's Newater recycling scheme and on transport operators' plans to increase fares on buses.

What does this suggest? That we will tolerate drinking water that has been urinated in but don't mess with us when it comes to white men and Singaporean women or you will really piss us off (pun intended)?

The SPG piece has been lauded for its honesty, despised for its "stereotypical comments"' and applauded for addressing a taboo subject in Singapore.

I have been warned by one irate writer that I should remember that "generalisations are dangerous" in Singapore. More dangerous, it would seem, than drinking recycled water.

She added that I am an expat who does not have a "housing allowance, much less a company car and definitely no fat wallet".

No arguments there but she hinted that this was because I was an "ugly bugger". A tad harsh, but it's true that I avoid job applications that state: "Ugly buggers need not apply".

The most perceptive criticism came from a Singaporean girl who had just returned from her studies in Britain. Understandably, she was critical of my claim that some Singaporeans return from the West with a touch of Western wannabe-itis. She wrote: "Mr. Humphreys, obviously male, is writing about female culture in Singapore — SPGs and what have you."

Well, I hold my hands up on that one. It is true that I am male; and in some aspects, "obviously so", though not in others, which is most unfortunate. So I suppose being male — that terrible, genetic failing of mine — must have had a subjective bearing upon my writing. Though the criticisms were most welcome, they were surprisingly few. The article certainly touched a nerve with so many Singaporeans.

One writer, obviously female, wrote: "I must say that your observation is something that most of us are embarrassed to talk about. It has become a norm to see a Singaporean girl-Western male couple. I've seen middle-aged Western guys with young Singaporean girls along Orchard Road, buying them branded stuff."

Well, who hasn't? And, according to some readers, it isn't just about money. One writer, who was also educated in Britain, wrote: "I guess some of them do it for the money. Many of them do it for what they imagine to be glamour. Little do these sad creatures know that back home, many *ang mohs* here are working-class individuals."

Another reader added: "Most local women don't realise that these *ang mohs* are your average Joe in England. They are only somebody in Singland, primarily because they are 'white' (no racist remark intended)."

None taken because, as I mentioned last week, I could name a handful of Caucasians who fall into that category, as could many other Singaporeans, it would seem.

It was interesting to see the situation from the other side of the fence. A Singaporean wrote: "My ex-girlfriend clearly suffers from the 'Western' syndrome, the details of which are too painful to put down in writing."

Of course, there were those who saw such "bitching" as a case of sour grapes. Letters arrived from people who are in happy inter-racial relationships, complaining that the article was too harsh. But even one of the sternest critics, on the subject of SPGs and Western wannabes, admitted: "That's not to say there aren't any. I know a few."

Don't we all? Judging by the overwhelming response from readers, many Singaporeans certainly do. That's the point. And, thankfully, it's hardly a taboo subject now. The can of worms has been spilt all over Emerald Hill. But then, would you rather talk about drinking water?

NOTE: Six months after the article and the subsequent reply came out — and I'm not making this up — my old friend Fran called me up and asked: "Did you say in the press that you wouldn't date a Singaporean woman?" Now this was a delicate issue, to say the least, because I've known Fran for years. And he's Canadian. And he's married to a Singaporean. But when I explained that I never said that at all, but merely commented on those who are only in it for the money and the social status, he was pacified. It transpired, though, that he'd been in Canada on vacation and when he'd returned, he heard a couple of colleagues refer to the article. Six months after it came out! It's bizarre. Nothing I have ever written before or since has touched a Singaporean nerve like the subject of inter-racial relationships. Funny, that.

THE DOCTOR

I DON'T like doctors. I didn't like them in England and, until recently, I didn't like them in Singapore. From the first time I heard the words, "You'll just feel a little prick in your bottom", I've viewed all forms of medical practice with a respectful distrust.

This uneasy relationship began when I was four years old. Sitting in the back of a delivery van with no seat belt on, my father hit the brakes sharply and I attempted, quite spontaneously, a Superman impression from a sitting position. The subsequent head injury required six stitches and my first ever tetanus injection.

Having been forced to expose my tender bottom to a rather buxom nurse (weren't they all, back then?), she whispered that immortal sentence involving "pricks" and "bottoms" for the first time. There was a slight pause, which allowed a builder to come in and insert a pneumatic drill up my arse.

Laying face down on the bed, my legs kicked out like a bucking horse, striking the terrified nurse in the chest. Though in truth, this was a difficult target to miss.

She jumped back clutching her breasts, I waddled off the bed with my trousers around my ankles like a petrified penguin and my mother slapped me for embarrassing her in a public place.

Since then, I have treated every successive visit to the doctor's surgery with mild apprehension, though my phobias of needles and breasts have subsided in recent years. But last week, the fear of all things clinical returned with a vengeance in the surreal waiting room of a doctor's surgery in Toa Payoh. My regular doctor, over in Lorong 8, was closed and I required urgent treatment for a brain tumour. What this hypochondriac really needed, of course, was a stronger pair of contact lenses and a deft blow to the head for wasting the doctor's time.

Luckily, I stumbled upon a doctor's surgery in Toa Payoh Central, which was still open. Two things should have struck me at this point. Firstly, how many private surgeries do you know that stay open after 8pm on a Saturday? Secondly, there was not a single patient in the waiting room, just two young receptionists watching a Chinese drama.

After registering at the counter, I started to read the posters in the waiting room. I was struck dumb with terror. My regular surgery had the usual warnings about vaccines for polio and hepatitis, but these were something else. For a start, they were handmade with marker pens and a stencil, which gave them a personal, homely touch. But the lines were jagged and shaky and I swore to myself that whoever the artist was, he would never be granted the opportunity to insert a needle in my bottom unless there was either an anaesthetic or copious amounts of vodka involved. Not that I was ever going to let myself be treated by a man who offered such a diverse, bizarre range of services.

On a single poster, he offered medical check-ups for work permits, hair replacement programmes, treatment for "sexual problems", medicine to improve the passage of stools and ear piercing! I pictured patients walking into the surgery, with some difficulty of course, and saying: "I've come to speed up my stool movement, not to mention my sex drive, and while I'm here, do you think you could put in these lovely diamond earrings because I'm going to a swanky dinner and dance." I'm sure she would look beautiful at the dinner, just make sure you're not caught sitting next to her when the stool potion kicks in.

If that wasn't enough, though, there was a printed poster next to the homemade efforts, which tackled the issue of herpes around the genitalia. Little was left to the imagination, but I'm afraid I'm going to leave it to yours. Let's just say there were enough graphic images of both men and women to put you off having sex — for the rest of your life.

Perhaps if the doctor offered a "set treatment", like a "set meal" at an economy rice stall, his waiting room would have more patients. Something like, one Viagra, a clear back passage, two earrings and free-flowing hair for 100 dollars.

The Chinese doctor was a most affable chap, who admitted that he specialised in cosmetic surgery, hence the unusual treatments and services on offer. But his surgery struck me as somewhat ironic. According to stereotype, Singaporeans are supposed to be the boring, ultra-conservative Asians and the British are supposed to be the gregarious, liberal Westerners. Yet every male member of my family, back in England, would cut his penis off before discussing his sex problems with a National Health Service doctor. In Toa Payoh, no discussion is even needed; one can point at poster A, B or C and say: "I've got that one there. The one with lots of weeping fluids."

I was so impressed by the openness of the surgery. After all, what is there to be ashamed of?

With National Day fast approaching, there is the usual talk of what it means to be a Singaporean, what makes a Singaporean a Singaporean and so on. Well, I propose that this Aug 9, we celebrate the unique and wonderful diversity of the average doctor's surgery in Singapore.

I'm no globetrotter, but I've visited enough countries to know that any medical establishment that can cure constipation and fix a receding hairline in one sitting is pretty special and a cause for celebration, surely. You don't think it will take off? Well, that's what cynics said about Viagra.

NOTE: The doctor's surgery is still there in Toa Payoh. Funnily enough, I've never been back since.

THE CROCODILE

CALL me a geek, but I visited the excellent Raffles Museum of Biodiversity Research recently. I went because I had read somewhere that old Stamford Raffles, Singapore's founder and British imperialist, was a bit of a naturalist. Rather excited by this, I went to the Museum at the National University of Singapore hoping to find lots of old oil paintings of Raffles in the buff and baring both cheeks for the artist.

Imagine the postcards one could send from Singapore. The two statues of the old Imperialist would have to be knocked down and two new *erections* would be in order. But, alas, Raffles the naturalist had a love for all things living and enjoyed cataloguing various plants and animals in his spare time. Apparently, he was fascinated by zoology and founded the famous London Zoo in Regents Park.

I'm sure all this nature talk is riveting, so allow me to reveal what I discovered at the Raffles Museum — there are still WILD CROCODILES IN SINGAPORE! Not baby ankle-biters that could give a nasty nip on your big toe, you understand, but two-metre-long buggers that can split you in two with a mere peck on the torso.

I bet that's got your attention, because it certainly got mine in the Raffles Museum. Noticing that estuarine crocodiles are indigenous to Southeast Asia, I said, as a joke, to one of the curators: "I saw one mauling a durian seller outside my block in Toa Payoh last week."

And he replied, almost casually: "Oh, we still find crocodiles in Singapore from time to time. An estuarine crocodile usually gets spotted once every few months in the wild."

I shit myself. It must be remembered that the housing estate I grew up on was not renowned for its wildlife. Two stray dogs mating beside a zebra crossing was about as exotic as it ever got.

Consequently, I still get excited when I see a gecko in the kitchen, but a crocodile is something else altogether. Estuarine crocodiles, would you believe, can grow up to 40 feet in length and favour mangrove-lined estuaries in this part of the world. Singapore's northern shore seems to be the preferred habitat for crocodiles. The Sungei Buloh Nature Park, with its wet, swampy environment, is a popular holiday destination for the bloody-thirsty reptile.

"Yes, we sometimes find crocodiles in Sungei Buloh," the curator told me casually, as if he was talking about crows being found at a hawker centre.

"In fact, one was photographed there in May 2002. It was only about two metres long. But it probably wasn't wild, it probably just escaped from a local crocodile farm."

This statement is most disconcerting for two reasons. Firstly, if it wasn't wild, how do you lose a two-metre long crocodile? When the crocodile farmer locks up for the night, surely he must say something like: "Right, final check: wallet, car keys, handphone and crocodiles. Hang on, where's Dorothy gone?"

But, more worryingly, were you convinced by the curator's reassurance that the crocodile "probably wasn't wild"? Does it really matter? It's not as if one is going to go paddling in a little stream near Kranji, spot the snout of a partially submerged Dorothy and say calmly: "It's okay dear. Don't panic, this crocodile's not wild. It's come from the farm. In fact, bring the kids and the camera down and we'll take a family photograph. Oh fuck, have you seen my leg?"

This is, of course, absolute nonsense. Should you spot a peckish Dorothy while out on a family picnic, run like hell and then change your underwear at the first opportunity. But seriously, the Singapore Tourism Board should be singing my praises for this wild discovery. Forget the Merlion spouting water, Singapore has crocodiles again. If it's good enough for tourists in the Australian outback, it's good enough for tourists here.

To substantiate my point, have you heard of Steve Irwin? He's that endearing, though clearly insane, crocodile hunter on the Discovery Channel. He might have more scars than Freddie Krueger, but he's an international celebrity now and a movie star to boot. More importantly, he has become a symbol for Australian tourism, just like Paul Hogan's Crocodile Dundee before him.

Now, Singaporeans can do the same. Let's have a Singapore Dundee. Prominent personalities and leading politicians could dress up in khaki safari suits and wear hats lined with crocodile teeth to promote this exotic metropolis. Overnight, it would transform the tourism trade into a billion-dollar industry.

In truth, nature lovers have about as much chance of

seeing a wild crocodile in Singapore as they have of spotting a tiger on Pulau Ubin. But Western tourists with fat, gullible wallets don't need to know that, do they?

Singapore already has monkeys and primary rainforest to rival Rio de Janeiro; now it can also boast two-metre crocodiles sneaking up its riverbanks. Forget the Northern Territory in Australia; the fierce creatures are here. Modern Singapore remains a wild island. After all, it was founded by a man who liked to run around baring his arse to the world. And life doesn't get any wilder than that.

NOTE: Shortly after this article came out, another crocodile was spotted doing a spot of breaststroke down at Sungei Buloh. I told you. The buggers are coming.

THE GRADUATION

WHEN I graduated from Manchester University, the degree ceremony resembled one of those prehistoric scenes in the BBC series *Walking with Beasts*. Like the primitive Neanderthals, those in attendance grunted, whooped and cheered every time a student went up to doth their mortarboards for the university's chancellor. By the time the occasion got into full swing, the grand hall witnessed chest-thumping, cartwheeling and chants of "you da man" — and that was just my mother.

The BBC's stunning depiction of early man is nothing compared to the ape-like behaviour of British parents celebrating their offspring's academic achievements. I was reminded of this recently, when I attended my first university graduation in Singapore.

As my girlfriend was one of the graduates, I felt obliged to attend and, besides, there was no football on TV that night.

Crammed into the ballroom at the Ritz-Carlton Hotel with 200 graduates and their families was, truly, an unforgettable experience. But then, so is an enema up the rectum.

A graduation ceremony, remember, is like a wedding — it's repetitive and poke-me-in-the-eye-with-a-chopstick boring. At a church wedding, we all "ooh" and "aah" in the right places and say "doesn't the groom look lovely in that white dress" (I've been to some liberal weddings), but what we're really doing is thinking about the food and alcohol back at the hotel reception.

Similarly, at a graduation, we clap politely as walking student gown No. 253 shakes hands with the chancellor and we wait — until our next of kin goes up on stage. Then, we stand up, take more photographs than the paparazzi and, then, we sit down again. That's how it's supposed to work — but no one told the irritating, impatient *kiasu* (literally meaning afraid to lose, in Hokkien) brigade this at the Ritz-Carlton.

As the chancellor called up the first batch of graduates, there was nothing. No cheering, no clapping, nothing. Apart from some stifled applauding, obviously from the graduates' families, there was virtual silence. There must have been 500 people in the room, yet the volume of applause was generated from no more than a handful of well-mannered folk.

Feeling the need to compensate, I began to resemble a performing sea lion. This caused the Chinese auntie next to me to stare at me. Her puzzled expression suggested she didn't know whether to laugh or throw me a fish. When it became apparent that I was merely clapping for strangers, she opted to laugh. So I hit her with my camcorder.

Before the ceremony started, a rather naive MC asked the audience: "Please stay seated, please do not block the middle aisle and please turn off your handphones."

The audience surpassed itself. Not only did it fail to comply with any of these polite requests, some of its more excited members managed to do all three at once. Before you could say "itchy backside", the audience was up and down more times than a convention for diarrhoea sufferers. The more adventurous *kiasus* actually left the ballroom, only to return, several minutes later, with plates of food that were supposed to be served only after the event had finished.

Kiasuism is an exhausting business, remember, which requires plenty of sustenance. The middle aisle, for instance, was meant to allow graduates to return to their seats. The organisers had even employed two Australians, with shoulders wider than the Singapore River, to keep the aisle pest-free.

They were the sort of muscle machines that could single-handedly keep 10,000 Melbourne maniacs away from Kylie Minogue. But the poor souls didn't stand a chance with the *kiasu* brigade. The area was soon besieged by hordes of enthusiastic, though very amateur, photographers. Graduates suffered the indignity of using their scrolls as *parangs* to cut a path through the crowd. And those who remained in their seats had their view obscured by countless, fidgety bottoms.

With my girlfriend's turn on stage fast approaching, I could see little more than one man's behind. So, like his damn camera, I snapped.

"Excuse me," I enquired. "Is this a lap dance club?"

"Huh?"

"Well, do you think I've paid 150 dollars to see the ceremony or your arse wiggling? And may I point out, you are no Kylie Minogue, so please sit down."

"Oh, sorry ah."

To his credit, he moved — a massive four centimetres to the left. In these tribal situations, of course, there must be leaders and there must be followers. Fortunately, there was a leader in the shape of a very prominent Singaporean politician, who had been invited to give the occasional address.

In my humble opinion, he had already completely cocked up his public performance by spilling water all over his speech notes. To compensate, he ad-libbed in a muffled voice for over half an hour. I've had wisdom tooth surgery that took less time.

During the on-going ceremony, however, the politician surpassed himself. He spent his time most productively — sending SMS text messages on his handphone, while sitting on the stage. What a role model for the proud graduates who walked past him unnoticed. Bring on the next courtesy campaign!

I tried to find the MP after the ceremony to discuss the importance of politicians practising what they preach, but he had gone. And, disastrously, so had all the *makan*. The *kiasu* brigade had eaten much of the food *during* the ceremony. In future, these occasions should come with a public health warning: "Eat before you go in and those who stick their buttocks into other people's faces risk a discreet elbow in the kidneys".

A celebration of academic achievement? Frankly, I'd rather sit through a convention for diarrhoea sufferers.

NOTE: Just to jog my memory, I watched my camcorder video of the graduation ceremony the other night. It's like sitting through a bad pornographic movie. The sound is really poor and every few minutes an arse pops into frame. Then it disappears; then it reappears. This goes on throughout the ceremony. And I was right about the guy's backside, too — a wide-screen TV wouldn't do it justice.

THE BREAK-DANCING

THE United Nations is clearly wasting its time. A workable solution to the Iraq crisis won't be found in peacekeeping soldiers wearing blue helmets in the Middle East. Instead, the answer has been found in Singaporean break-dancers wearing bandanas at Far East Plaza.

One Saturday afternoon, I inadvertently found myself in the basement of the shopping mall, which now poses as the labyrinth of cool. It has become a mini-funky town of hip clothes, music and pop culture, generally. Teenagers with model looks who personify sophistication stand outside the shops looking devastatingly handsome.

Yes, fair enough, I found it by accident and was about to leave when the PA system announced a dancing exhibition to promote some trendy camera the size of a thumbnail. You hang the camera around your neck like a pendant. The idea being, I suppose, that you never know when you are going to get caught stranded on a desert island. This way you can take photographs of your environment so that, when your body is found, your relatives will have some souvenirs from your final days.

Several elderly aunties, who had either bought one of the cameras or, like me, were clearly in the wrong place, were heading for the escalator when they started cooing excitedly.

"Wait *lah*," said the apparent leader of the group. "Watch dancing first. Come we go near the front. Can see better from there."

Quite obviously, they were expecting a ballroom dancing display or a line dancing routine perhaps with a group of well-rehearsed senior citizens wearing cowboy costumes. And then seven youngsters came out, wearing jeans that would have been too baggy for Coco the Clown, and started spinning on their heads. It was truly priceless. The aunties' faces transformed from a kind of eager expectation to a kind of "what the fuck is this?" expression. The music was so loud that the baselines made the floors vibrate — in Toa Payoh. There was robotic body-popping, head and body spinning, back flips and cartwheels and the occasional shout of "Let's go, you mothers!" And that was just the aunties.

But I thought I'd been transported back to my childhood. When it was 1982 and lots of electric boogaloo. Break-dancing was the thing to do. And I couldn't do it. Attempts to do the caterpillar across the living room floor often culminated in my lanky legs flipping up and kicking me in the back of the head. My mother would then slap me for blocking the television and I would promptly pass out.

Yet, here we were in Far East Plaza in 2003 and break-dancing was back and it was happening. One of the younger aunties had even started to clap along with the frantic hyper base throbbing. Initially, she appeared to be waiting for Engelbert Humperdinck to come out and start crooning, "Please Release Me". But now, I half expected her to turn her cap around, somersault across the floor, high-five the other funky dancers and join in. When the rather impressive exhibition had finished, there was generous applause from a 200-strong crowd while the eager auntie pumped her fist and shouted, "woo, woo, woo," as the performers left the stage.

After the show, I had a chat with the dancers and they spoke to me like I was mentally ill. They told me break-dancing had been dead since the '80s, but now it was making a comeback as part of the hip-hop culture. And who's part of the hip-hop culture, I asked 17-year-old Gianna. These guys were strictly one-name people.

"Oh, it's guys like Eminem and Missy Elliot."

"Miss C who?" She looked at me with benign pity, as if I needed help to cross the road. Or my incontinence knickers needed changing perhaps.

"Missy Elliot? The singer? You know who she is right?"

"What? Me and Miss C? Are you kidding? I've got so many of her albums, we're almost friends. She is up there, man. Miss C is up there with M C Hammer and Vanilla Ice."

I felt 128 years old.

The break-dancers called themselves Radikal Forze, with a 'K' and a 'Z' no less. There were seven of them — five Malays, one Chinese and one Caucasian and their ages ranged from 14 to 36. Being the minority, I asked National Serviceman Felix if he felt like an outsider.

"No way, man," the Chinese teenager told this 'man'. "We come from different races and different backgrounds. But we just work and practise together because we love what we do. There are no barriers, man."

And that's when I realised that Felix is right and the United Nations is wrong. In the '80s, conflicts and disputes between rival gangs on the streets of New York were often settled through break-dancing. There were movies and documentaries about it. A body-popping contest, or 'burn', to use its street name, would be held and two enemies would attempt to out-dance the other into submission.

When I was 11 years old, the school bully summoned me to 'burn' with him in the playground. It was spectacularly awful. Neither of us could perform any dance moves, except the 'arm caterpillar'. Do you remember that one? You just flicked your left arm like a caterpillar and moved through to the right arm in one fluid motion. Well, we stood chest-to-chest and did the 'arm caterpillar'. For an hour. Until the bell went. In the afternoon, neither of us could lift our arms, except when they involuntarily flicked into the 'arm caterpillar'. The spasms were most inconvenient. The history teacher kept assuming we were putting our hands up, in rather extravagant fashion, to answer questions on Stalinist Russia.

And that brings me back to current dictators with moustaches. That 'burn' between the bully and myself was a success in the sense that we left each other alone after that. So if it worked for schoolboys, it'd certainly work for George Bush and Saddam Hussein, wouldn't it?

Get them both down to the United Nations' headquarters (Bush will cry and tell his daddy if he doesn't have home advantage) and send out Radikal Forze with both their 'K' and 'Z' to train the two leaders.

Then, before the world's news cameras, Missy Elliot could bang out a few tunes and Bush and Saddam could stick out their chests in that belligerent pose popular with world leaders and totalitarian pretenders and get to work on the 'arm caterpillar'. Once the 'burn' has reached a satisfactory conclusion, the schoolboy-cum-national leaders must thrash out their differences. Incidentally, has anyone else noticed that if you say Saddam backwards, it comes out as 'mad ass'?

Now, you may think I'm naive and out-of-touch (the break-dancers certainly did), but wouldn't it be rather wonderful if we could solve global disputes with body-popping, rather than gun-popping?

THE GEEK

MY missus has seriously contemplated leaving me recently. And I know precisely where and why it happened. We were at the Kranji Reservoir, a beautiful green spot that overlooks Malaysia in the north of Singapore, when I heard a distinct rustling in the long reeds hanging over the edge of the bank. A bird had landed. Not just any bird, you understand, but a grey heron. With no time to lose and absolutely no thought for my own safety, I dashed off in pursuit. Stopping some 10 metres from the long-legged bird to compose myself (and I haven't done that since I last frequented the tacky nightclubs of my youth in Essex), I crouched down to allow the long grass to provide some natural cover.

And then, the bird looked up at me. Quickly but calmly, I reached for my trusty pocket book, entitled *A Guide To The Common Birds Of Singapore*, and sought out my tasty bird. Well, I just could not contain myself.

"It's not a common heron, mate," I shouted to the missus. "The beak is black. It could well be a little egret. Hang on, I'll get a bit closer and compare the photographs."

"Neil!" came the rather urgent reply.

"Yes, mate?"

"You look a complete fucking wanker."

"Yes, mate." Her comments threw me off kilter slightly. She rarely called me names, well, not in public at least. Luckily, at a largely deserted Kranji Reservoir on a Sunday afternoon, there are usually only teenaged courting couples eating each other on the benches. Their only concern is whether or not they can get away with a quick shag in the park without being spotted by a passer-by, an *ang moh* amateur ornithologist or, worse still, their parents. So I knew I hadn't suffered public humiliation. But the unnecessary swearing rankled a little. I mean, I'd been called a wanker by various members of my girlfriend's family more times than I care to remember. But the f-word meant she was somewhat perturbed. This was hardly a trifling matter.

"What was all that about?" I asked, adopting my best hangdog face. It never works, though; I always come off more like a rabid dog.

"What the fuck are you doing getting on your hands and knees and making a tit of yourself for?" God, I love her. You don't get brutal honesty like that from the snotty-nosed types in the wealthy suburbs of England.

"I was looking for wild birds, weren't I? You knew that. That's why we came here in the first place, didn't we?"

"No, you said we were going to look for some wildlife. That's fine. I didn't expect you to roll around in the mud, looking at pigeons."

"It's an egret."

"I couldn't give a shit what it was. You look bloody stupid."

And then I saw another exotic bird swoop down and land beside the egret/heron and I lost my senses. My missus, on the other hand, lost the will to live.

"Shit. There's another one," I shouted and ran off again. But my excitement superceded my concentration and the sound of a red-faced Caucasian stumbling through the reeds terrified my birds and they flew off into the trees. Now, it was the wanker's chance to retaliate.

"Are you happy now, you stupid woman? They've gone. That's it. I'm buying a pair of binoculars and not some cheap kiddy's pair neither. I'm getting a decent pair like ornithologists use."

She looked at me, throughly horrified. Initially, my little rant had rendered her speechless before she managed to compose herself.

"Wait a minute," she said. "You want to buy a pair of binoculars so you can sit under a tree for hours looking for birds?"

"That's right. I don't sound too silly now, do I?"

"Look, mate," she replied calmly. "If you buy those binoculars, you will never be the father of my children."

She was only joking. At least, I hope she was because I really fancy a pair of binoculars. But seriously, she was right. What have I become? What has Singapore done to me? I'd become a wildlife geek — one of those weedy, bookworm types that parents would make their children avoid on buses when I was growing up in England. Living on the working-class council estate of Dagenham, the only animals I ever saw came in batter next to my chips. That was the perfect symbiotic relationship as far as I was concerned.

But Singapore has irrevocably changed that ignorant perception towards my fellow earthly species forever. During that weekend when I went heron hunting, we encountered monkeys at Bukit Timah Nature Reserve and Pierce Reservoir, a couple of sizable monitor lizards at Lower Seletar Reservoir and then came the icing on the geek's cake.

Having a well-deserved break at Lower Seletar, we were sitting in front of the catchment area admiring the view when we witnessed something straight out of a documentary for the Discovery Channel. I noticed a bird (I feel like such a sad twat when I know that you now know, instinctively, that I am referring to the feathered variety) circling above the water. It was certainly a bird of prey and, on closer inspection, I realised it was a kite.

Now, before you laugh, I went to Australia last year and they were all over the Northern Territory there so they're easy to spot. Then, suddenly, just as I was about to divulge the feeding habits of the kite to the missus, the brown beast stretched out its talons and swooped towards the surface of the water. The huge claws went below the surface and came out swiftly bearing a rather stunned fish. Despite the fish being over half the size of the kite and wriggling like a lunatic, the kite gamely held on and took its supper back to the trees. Not 10 metres away, incidentally, stood a rather nonplussed fisherman, who boasted rather expensive fishing equipment, but had caught nothing other than a decent suntan. At times, nature has a wonderful way of reminding man of his real place in the world.

Moments like that have not only given me a greater appreciation of living in Southeast Asia, but have also fueled my rather geeky obsession with wildlife and ecosystems. Singaporeans, particularly those who've completed their national service in the few remaining jungles and rainforests around the Republic, are probably wondering what the big deal is. A bird catching his dinner? That sounds riveting. Do you remember what time it was so we can choose our 4-D lottery numbers?

But you must put it into context. I grew up in Dagenham. A tiny London borough full of endless, monotonous rows of red-bricked council houses. The only exotic wildlife I ever saw was on the BBC, which showed documentaries often made in South-east Asia. That could have been 10 miles from Jupiter for all I cared. The only wild animal that I ever saw was my mother when I was 17. My girlfriend's extremely forgiving parents brought my drunk body home to my mother one night and she turned into some sort of chimera and proceeded to batter me for the next two hours for embarrassing her in front of strangers.

In Dagenham, a stray dog could stop the traffic. Drivers would stare at the beast in the same way that village idiots of medieval times used to come out of their huts and take their dunce caps off to point at the moon. But my apathy towards animals came about after living with two of the stupidest animals since the dinosaurs looked up at the meteors, nudged each other and said: "It's all right, John. It's just a passing shower." My first dog, Duke, enjoyed pissing on the legs of fellow dog owners at my local park. On one occasion, a burly man with a urine-soaked trouser leg chased me in retaliation. It's probably the only time a 12-year-old boy has outrun a Doberman.

My second dog, Bruno, went blind at a very young age, which was tragic. What is far more tragic, however, is the perverse sense of fun the family still has from watching my mad mother throw sticks for the poor dog, who then spends the next 15 minutes not finding any of them.

So, before I came to Singapore, my appreciation and recognition of my fellow species never went beyond the odd nature programme and tying Duke to the garden fence and forcing him to play goalkeeper. The bastard dog still won most of the penalty shootouts.

Therefore, my transformation has been nothing short of remarkable. I now think I'm Southeast Asia's answer to David Attenborough. And yet, of course, there is a certain irony to all of this. Outsiders, and insiders for that matter, perceive this tiny city-state to be the archetypal concrete jungle. Like Dagenham, Singapore's skyline is punctuated with unremarkable municipal housing blocks. There is little variety in terms of shape, design and colour and they have largely swallowed up the greenery that once covered the land. The town planners of the London County Council dug up the peaceful farmlands of Dagenham in the '20s. Forty years later, the HDB planners were cutting down the Asian rainforests here. The only difference was, once the bulldozing had finished, Dagenham didn't continue to breed lizards, monkeys, lemurs, pythons, cobras, the odd wild boar, the occasional crocodile and, last but not least, kites, herons, eagles and egrets.

Unfortunately, my first encounter with a wild mammal was an underwhelming experience, to say the least. Having been in Singapore for about a week, I went to the bottom of the HDB block to make a call. Not only did I arrive in the country without the customary expatriate package (condo, car, maid, Singapore Cricket Club membership), I didn't even have a phone. It was around midnight and I was chatting to my girlfriend when I abruptly interrupted her with the gentle cry of: "FUCK ME! IT'S A RAT."

Believe it or not, it was the first rat I'd ever seen. Despite growing up near the London Underground tube lines (a popular holiday destination for the little bastards), we had never had a formal introduction. But my phobia of rodents is primal. It goes right to my soul, or arsehole if you will. It's hereditary and the fear comes from my mother, reinforced by a couple of incidents that will have you screaming in your sleep tonight. Just listen to this. When I was 11, I returned from the cub scouts, starving as usual, and my mother informed me that there was some soup in a saucepan on the cooker. As I touched the handle, a gluttonous mouse jumped out of the saucepan, having consumed its weight in soup first, ran along the sideboard and disappeared. That was terrifying enough. But the soup was tomato. The rodent, which was more Fat Bastard than Stuart Little, jumped out of the pan drenched in soup and staggered away like a hairy tomato, leaving little blood-red footprints along the way.

But there's more. And this one will put you off your dinner. About a year later, my mother cooked us roast potatoes one night and kept cooking oil, or lard, in the baking tray and left it to solidify overnight. This was a common way of recycling the oil and saving a few pennies. However, the next day my mother opened the oven, lifted out the baking tray, screamed and, then, promptly dropped it. You see, an adventurous young mouse allowed greed to supercede his common sense. Nipping through the back of the oven for a little tipple of lard, the obese bugger didn't take the hint when the temperature started to cool. Consequently, the oil solidified and he inadvertently got trapped. And my mother found him the next day: suffocated, extremely stiff and trying to perfect the spreadeagled pose in death.

Unsurprisingly, I seriously contemplated leaving Singapore that night. Living among mice in London was horrifying enough, living with their Asian big brother was a different gang of rodents altogether. I actually made enquiries about the extent of the rat population here. Such as which parts of the country they favoured, what their dietary habits were and whether or not I could be arrested for firebombing every sewer in Toa Payoh. However, they actually bother me far less now and I seldom see them. When I first moved here, there was upgrading work everywhere and now that's finished, many have had to relocate to some of the condos being constructed out in the East Coast.

But my run-in with king rat was, admittedly, an inauspicious start to my wildlife expeditions in Southeast Asia. Fortunately, I stumbled upon the Bukit Timah Nature Reserve after about three months and watched, transfixed, for hours as a long-tailed macaque skillfully cleaned its offspring of fleas, in a tender, maternal fashion. And I was hooked. Sublime incidents like that had a profound effect on me and the missus, who actually became a vegetarian as a result.

At the risk of sounding like an anally retentive presenter from the Discovery Channel, I have to admit that living here has forced me to develop a greater respect for the various ecosystems and all of their components, having seen many of them in action.

At Bukit Timah, I sat for 15 minutes and watched intensely as a monitor lizard burrowed its snout deep into the soil in a rhythmic fashion, not quite sure whether it was searching for food or merely picking his nose using an obscure prehistoric method. But then, the reptile snapped its head back sharply, pulling a worm from the ground and throwing it into the air in one fluid motion. Within milliseconds, it had caught its dinner and was chewing away quite happily. I waited patiently for another few minutes, but crocodile hunter Steve Irwin never jumped out and shouted: "Did you see that? What a beauty. Woo!"

At Sungei Buloh, I saw a monitor lizard swim for the first time. This was a rather hair-raising incident for three reasons. Firstly, I didn't know monitor lizards could swim. Yes, I know I'm ignorant. Didn't you hear where I grew up? Secondly, I assumed it must have been a crocodile because I know they can swim. Thirdly, crocodiles eat people. When I was a kid, I used to watch the James Bond movie *Live And Let Die* endlessly. There's a famous scene in the film where Roger Moore has to run across the backs of several crocodiles to escape. I thought I was going to have to do the same at Sungei Buloh. That's no way to die. Can you imagine the headlines? "ANG MOH WRITER DIES AFTER USING MIDGET CROCODILE AS A SURFBOARD" — there's no disgrace in dying at the jaws of a beast that has been around since the age of dinosaurs, but it can be a trifle embarrassing to go down to a crocodile that suffered from stunted growth.

But the real wildlife highlight was catching two lizards shagging. The young reptiles couldn't have been more than 25 centimetres long, but length isn't everything. They didn't need any patronising government campaign on love and romance, I can assure you. Playing tennis at the time, I went to the back of the court to collect some balls and found a couple more than I expected. Right on the doubles line were two little love-makers going through the lizard *Kama Sutra*.

It was spectacular. I dropped my racket and sat beside them and watched, fascinated. My only regret was I didn't have popcorn for the matinee performance. I called my tennis part-ner over to have a look, but he muttered something like "Fuck me, it'll be farmyard animals next, the filthy bastard," and then said he had to stop by the local police post to report some pervert.

I don't know what he was going on about. But I was mesmerised. I'd seen plenty of stray dogs having sex on the way home from school. And I caught a few bare arses going up and down in the back seats of Ford Cortinas over my local park after late football matches. But the only fucking reptiles I'd ever seen in England sat in Parliament in Westminster. So I hope you can appreciate how truly happy I was sitting on the floor of a sun-baked tennis court observing two lizards performing an act that often requires a night out, copious amounts of alcohol and three hours of begging before two humans have a bash at it.

After that life-altering experience, I've become an eco-tourism addict. I won't go anywhere now unless there is wildlife involved. Trekking in Langkawi's rainforests in Malaysia, we witnessed a full-scale monkey brawl as two sides fought viciously before retreating to opposite sides of the path to check their injuries. It was like a monkey audition for *West Side Story*.

In Western Australia, we got up close to southern right whales who were heading up the coast of the country towards their annual breeding grounds. In an isolated spot in Indonesia's Bintan Island, I spotted a family of wild boars out for a pint at a deserted stream.

On another occasion, in Bintan, I was sitting on a bus when an elephant walked past the window. Admittedly, it wasn't wild. But think about it. How often does Dumbo go past your window when you're sitting in a traffic jam?

In England, the only mammals that approach your windows at traffic lights are the human kind, who wash your windscreen, whether it needs cleaning or not, and demand payment when they are finished. Give me a cumbersome elephant every time. I wouldn't have been impersonating Daft Attenborough in any of these places had it not been for the tiny, so-called concrete jungle that I'm now living in.

And then, the little-known village of Chek Jawa made the headlines and I wanted to punch every *kiasu*, small-minded, short-sighted politician and prick in Singapore. Tucked away in the far-eastern corner of Pulau Ubin were the rich sand and mud flats of Chek Jawa. It was hidden behind an old British bungalow and was largely ignored by nature lovers and tourists because of high tides. Then, in late 2000, old homes of the island's villagers were destroyed in preparation for land reclamation. And the path was open for intrepid wildlife explorers to find, well, everything. This mini-coastal forest had mangroves, a lagoon, coral rubble and hitherto rarely discovered marine and wildlife. The Nodular Sea Star, flower crabs, hornbills, the hairy Heavy Jumper spider (it looks a bit like a tarantula and I just love the name), the dog-toothed cat snake (again, what a name), the Banded Bullfrog and the good old wild boar are just some of the residents of Chek Jawa. Believe me, there are dozens more.

The discoveries of so many wonderfully varied ecosystems (six, in fact) seemed almost too good to be true. Singapore had found a new Eden within its narrow borders. But they were to lose it again. The bulldozers were ready to go in and rip it up. The government, via the Urban Redevelopment Authority, had decided in the revised Concept Plan of 2001 that the eastern coastline could be spared for land reclamation. Do you know what the land was going to be used for? New HDB flats? Schools? Hospitals perhaps? Of course not. The plan was to create land for military training. That's right. Either experienced soldiers would run around the place shooting things and blowing other things up. Or inexperienced teenagers, performing their National Service duties, would miss targets and such things initially, before blowing things up at the second attempt. And then the government has the audacity to brand people "quitters" for seeking, in many cases, to give their children a more wholesome, varied upbringing in another country.

Can you imagine taking your grandchild to Chek Jawa in 20 years and the young boy saying: "Granddad, what are all those explosions banging over there? And why are there huge fences and 'KEEP OUT OR WE'LL BLOW YOUR FUCKING HEAD OFF' signs everywhere?" What could you say to that? Perhaps you could sit the innocent boy on your knee and say: "Well, this was once a paradise, son, full of the kind of wildlife you now only see in zoos. Animals, fish, trees and seagrasses everywhere. It was stunning. Now, there are teenagers dressed in green camouflage, running around with machine guns shooting, er, things."

"I think I prefer it the way before, Granddad." We should fill parliaments with children. They don't bullshit each other. They haven't been engulfed by cynicism and, in their simplicity, they speak, at times, with a profound wisdom. But we don't. So we're stuck with the middle-aged cynics. However with the Chek Jawa issue, they came unstuck. This one couldn't be swept under the mud flats, as it were. There was considerable protest.

In England, this would involve 100,000 nature lovers marching around the streets of Westminster with placards. Here, that is not allowed, so there were several strongly worded letters to the Forum pages instead. Sometimes, politicians here forget who elects whom. Fortunately, on this occasion, there was not

49

a shortage of wonderful Singaporeans eager to remind them. The researchers and volunteers from the outstanding Raffles Museum of Biodiversity Research and the Nature Society of Singapore just refused to go away. They undertook surveys and, despite limited resources, recorded an impressive list of species that could be lost forever. It was a death list.

In the wake of such vehement protest, the government relented, albeit temporarily. In late December 2001, just days before the bulldozers were about to go in, the official reprieve came. The Chek Jawa beach would be left intact — for 10 years. But the fact remains that if the government then decides that land is needed, then that will take priority, of course, over some daft multi-coloured fish and some crabs with silly names that would look much better on a plate with a bit of chilli anyway, right?

Forgive me if I don't shit myself with excitement at the news that Chek Jawa has been spared. You see, when the news broke that the rural haven was about to be destroyed, Singaporeans were encouraged to see for themselves just what they would be taking away from their children. Many turned up, in their thousands, in fact, which was truly amazing for a so-called apathetic nation.

But some brought carrier bags. This wasn't a nature expedition. It was a treasure hunt. Seriously distressed guides tried in vain to stop many taking sea urchins, sea cucumbers, starfish, seagrasses and even fish as souvenirs. Ridiculous trinkets from Chek Jawa. Marine life was actually taken out of the sea and suffocated just so it could pose for a family snapshot. When the carrier-bag brigade left, the beach was strewn with dead species. Ironically, these fuckwits were killing the very ecosystems that more sensible people were fighting to save. In the current age of environmental awareness and appreciation, this ignorance is not just exasperating; it's bloody terrifying.

And you know, you just know, that these are the same *kiasus* who sit around and whine that "Singapore is so boring" and they have to pay thousands to take their children to Sea World to watch a dolphin jump through a hoop. And they tell me to visit Malaysia and Indonesia if I want wildlife. Why? It's here in abundance. For a country so small and urbanised, it is remarkable how much wildlife the Republic still has. But how much more needs to be wiped out, before Singaporeans say: "Shit, maybe this country really will be soulless and boring if all we have left are people, handphones, golf courses and concrete." The tiger has already gone, which is probably just as well because some *kiasu* cab driver would knock him down in Orchard Road. The beast's testicles would be removed before you could say: "You know, there is Viagra for that medical condition now. Those bloody testicles you are holding would work much better on the tiger, don't you think? You prick."

Of course, Singapore isn't Brazil. It's not Yellowstone Park, the Serengeti or even Sarawak or Borneo, but it's the wildest city I've ever known and not just because of the availability of hookers. Just recently, for instance, I was at the Lower Pierce Reservoir at dusk, my favourite time of the day in Singapore. Walking along the water's edge, we came across members of the nature society. There were around 20 of them, all pointing and gesturing frantically towards a tree opposite them. It was a barn owl. A huge bugger, in fact. I almost wet myself with excitement. One of the society's members lent me his binoculars so I could see right into the owl's eyes. I started jumping around like a big kid. That's when the missus decided to pipe up: "You really are a wanker, aren't you?"

And she's right. In Dagenham-speak, I am a sad wanker and proud of it. You should be too. So put this book down, grab a pair of binoculars and explore the island for yourself. There's plenty to see in Singapore, more than enough to go around. It's bloody marvellous.

THE TOILET

USUALLY, I would not resort to toilet humour, but on this occasion I believe I have found the answer to one of Mr. Goh Chok Tong's problems. The Singapore Prime Minister knows that his residents are migrating in droves to Australia — that financial oasis with cut-price suburban houses, cheap cars and kangaroo poo everywhere. He is trying to convince the "quitters" to remain with the loyal "stayers", but this is no easy task.

The brain drain is a real headache for the Prime Minister. But, fear not, because I have found the answer — Australian public toilets. These "amenities" are the most irritating, most expensive and most bewildering on the planet. Collectively, they should provide a deterrent to all Singaporeans who are considering settling Down Under.

Having just returned from Australia, I speak from bitter experience on this one. The reason why properties there are so cheap is because you have to take out a second mortgage to use a public toilet. Every trip costs a whopping 50 cents. Only 50 cents, you say? This is the middle of the Alice Springs desert, where large quantities of water are essential to stay alive.

I was using the little boys' room more often than George Michael. It was costing me three dollars a day and that didn't even include those cute packets of tissues given out in Singapore. When it reached the stage where my wallet had to make a choice between urinating and eating, I headed for the local K-Mart supermarket. Surely the facilities would be free there? Indeed they were, but they were locked — deliberately. Frantic and cross-legged, I asked a girl at the checkout if they were being cleaned.

"No," she replied. "You can get the key from me."

"What key?"

"The key to the toilet. And could you please bring it back when you're finished."

Bring it back? What the hell did she think I was going to do with a key to a K-Mart public toilet? Pretend it was an Aussie souvenir and send it to my mother? Though, in truth, if I stuck a magnet on the back of it, she'd happily stick it on the fridge.

In the end, the thought of carrying a large toilet key around a supermarket was just too embarrassing. I hadn't even bought anything. So I headed back to the "we-rip-off-bladder-bursting-men" establishment.

Slightly perturbed that the 50 cents didn't include piped music, light refreshments and a full massage from a Swedish sex siren, I asked the chain-smoking attendant why: a) most public amenities were locked and b) why the rest cost a small fortune.

"Aborigines," she replied. "If we don't charge or lock up, they defecate on the floor and vomit up the walls. Some even go in to sleep. I wouldn't like to think about the amount of diseases that must be in that toilet." And then the ignorant woman took my 50 cents and blew smoke in my face. Now, has that put you off emigrating yet?

The only negative experiences I have had in a Singaporean urinal involved being watched by a disturbingly zealous cleaner. Many times I have asked the female toilet cleaner at my office if I might relieve myself, only to find her still cleaning the floor behind me. I had expected her to wait outside. But no, she decides that the spot right by my feet, which is shockingly close to my exposed testicles, must be cleaned at that exact moment.

I have also cut a path to several toilets at hawker centres — an expedition which required side-stepping the unwashed plates of *mee goreng*, hopping over the cigarette cartons and sliding along various liquids of an unknown origin. It was only the absence of a giant, concrete ball that prevented me from resembling an incontinent Indiana Jones.

But these public antiquities are in rapid decline and will soon be replaced completely by those state-of-the-art amenities in most shopping centres. Yet, be careful; these could become a dangerous social menace. PM Goh suggested recently that if Singaporeans are to succeed, they must become more self-reliant. These modern toilets encourage anything but self-reliance. Recently, I went to a toilet that flushed the urinal for me, dried my hands automatically and, wait for it, released water from the tap without touching it.

Just putting my hands under the tap's censor did the trick. Now, I know we need to conserve water, but this is ridiculous. I appreciate the "Keep toilets clean" campaigns and their importance, but, surely, Singaporeans can turn a tap on for themselves. I've met some loonies in Toa Payoh, but not even they would go up to a tap and say: "Now, this must be the dimmer switch for the lights."

Whatever next? Perhaps plumbers will install a magnetic contraption above the urinal, which automatically undoes the zip on your trousers? That might be worth 50 cents.

Until then, let's demonstrate remarkable self-reliance and stupendous multi-tasking skills by flushing our own toilets and washing our own hands.

Believe me, it's a better alternative than going up to a supermarket cashier and asking for an oversized toilet key like a guilty schoolboy. But if we really want to curb Singaporean migrations to Australia, then I would seriously urge the government to consider that magnetic zip idea.

NOTE: I received an irate email concerning this article, from a man who thought I was trivialising the stayer-quitter emigration debate in Singapore. He reminded me, quite forcefully, that the state of a country's public toilets is not high on the list of priorities for potential emigrants. This wasn't an issue, he claimed, that would affect 'normal' people. I tried to picture these 'normal' people, but I quickly stopped. They were starting to scare me. Nevertheless, I thanked him for his email and for pointing out that the majority of Singaporeans don't have public urinals on their minds when they are choosing what country to spend the rest of their lives in. Of course, what I really wanted to say was: "Please, please let me pay your airfare to Australia and don't ever return to Singapore again, you sad bastard." But I didn't.

THE GAMES

SINGAPOREAN killjoys ruined the Asian Games 2002 celebrations. Despite the five gold medals won by the Republic, there were still pessimists on hand to cheapen the achievements of its bowlers and bodybuilders. And that's tragic.

It's not easy to knock down 10 milk bottles with a plastic cannonball, you know. It's no small feat to slip on a pair of skimpy Speedos and strike a pose without slipping in all that cooking oil that has been smeared all over their bodies either. Bodybuilders are under intense pressure to ensure that they bulge in all the right places — especially as they are only wearing a pair of skimpy Speedos. There are no extra points awarded for that muscle. And we shouldn't even consider what sort of training programme it would require.

But no one should downplay these sporting accomplishments, particularly when they bring the medals in at such a prestigious continental competition. In fact, why stop there? Let's exercise cool calculation rather than sporting snobbery and petition the Olympic Council Asia (OCA) to include other widely practised "sports".

According to the OCA, a sport must have a high participation rate to be considered for inclusion in the Asian Games. That being the case, I humbly nominate the sport of queuing. By definition, it requires mass participation and Singaporeans have turned it into an art form.

Queuing encourages Sports-For-All and collectivism, which will keep the government happy. It is also cheap. Unlike elitist sports such as horseracing and sailing, queuing equipment can be afforded by just about everybody. A singlet, loose-fitting shorts and a pair of flip-flops should guarantee maximum performance.

Like a melodrama made for the Hallmark Channel, children would sit on their mother's knee, look up in admiration and say: "Mummy, when I grow up, I wanna be like you. I want to queue, too. But I don't want to do it just for a cheap quilt with matching pillow and bolster cases; I want to do it for my country. Mummy, I want to queue for Singapore!"

Regional queuers could congregate at the National Stadium for the referee to announce: "On your marks, get set, HDB flats for sale!" The last, sleep-starved person who remains upright wins the race. It might not measure up as a spectator sport, but consider the medal potential for Singapore.

The same could be said for the sport of queens. And when I say queens, I mean talking aunties. Put any Singaporean woman over the age of 60 on a bus. Tell her to talk, incessantly, on any subject she likes and I guarantee she will shut out all competition, quite literally. Foreign aunties would be screaming for an oxygen tank before any Singaporean woman finally stops talking. Though the English old lady would run her a close second, I must admit.

The referee could stand between them and shout: "On your marks, get set, gossip!" to begin the inane conversation. Incorporating the three-strikes-and-you're-out rule, the jabbering aunties should be supplied with three prompts if the chatter starts to flag. At intervals, the referee could shout subjects like: "food", "noisy neighbours" and "grandchildren" to keep the contest going.

Be warned, though. Singaporean aunties have a tendency to disagree, whereas their English counterparts love to agree with everything. So the final talk-out could well consist of: "Grandchildren? Cannot tahan. No, no, no, no, no."

"Ooh, I know."

"Very naughty one."

"Ooh, I know."

"Kids today; no discipline."

"Ooh, I know."

"No, cannot. No, no, no, no, no."

"Ooh, I know." It would be riveting stuff.

However, if you're looking for a testosterone-charged, pumped-up, adrenaline-filled extravaganza, then you might consider the 4 x 100-metre bookie runners' relay. Using their handphones as a baton, four illegal bookies would settle in the starting blocks, wearing the appropriate sporting attire — a singlet, loose-fitting shorts and flip-flops. The race referee would then cry: "On your marks, get set, Manchester United half ball!"

To make it a fair contest, the illegal runners must all natter continuously into their handphones to take bets, check the form-guide and discuss their upcoming court cases. Even if they didn't win the race (they'd face strong opposition from the gambling Thais), they'd make a few dollars by the time they crossed the finish line. Indeed, money and sport are intrinsically linked in the modern era so there's every reason to include illegal VCD sellers at the next Asian Games.

Weightlifting already has the 'clean and jerk' and 'snatch' categories, which are pretty vague to most sports fans. Initially, I thought they involved pornography. I'm almost certain you need to do one before the other anyway. But Singaporeans should petition for slight variations — the 'jerks, clean and pack' swiftly followed by the 'snatch the cash'.

Training funds would not be required from the Singapore Sports Council — experienced *ah bengs* are fully trained. The sport's set up is simple enough. Two competitors (from Woodlands and Johor Baru, respectively) would warm up behind two old wooden tables full of illegal VCDs. Their strict training regime usually involves furtive glances along the street and continuous smoking.

The athletes could perform in whatever they feel comfortable in — though a singlet, loose-fitting shorts and flip-flops appear to be remarkably popular. Then, the referee could mutter: "On your marks, get set, *aiyoh*, CID!"

In such situations, *ah bengs* demonstrate quicker reflexes than any martial arts exponent. The jerks can clean the table and pack away the VCDs before you can say: "Was that the Pamela Anderson-Tommy Lee home video?" The first athlete to then grab the box, snatch the cash and sprint away wins the gold. The defeated opponent, however, must settle for silver and six months in Changi prison.

Nevertheless, with these new sports added to the Asian Games' schedule, Singapore could easily become the most bemedalled country in the region. If nothing else, imagine what these additions could do for the local flip-flop industry.

NOTE: A friend of mine, who works at the Singapore Sports Council, said this column was well received around the office. I expect to be made SSC chairman any day now.

THE DANCE

UNLIKE those Coyote Ugly beauties down at Mohammed Sultan Road, I can't dance. On a good night, I look like a break-dancing C3PO with rusty joints. Such talents are hereditary. My father was famous (in his house) for his Michael Jackson moonwalk. After his seventh beer, I would hear: "Come and see this, son. I taught Michael Jackson everything he knows. Watch this moonwalk."

"Dad," I would reply. "You're just walking backwards."

"No, son, look and learn from the white man who taught the black man. Now, watch the Jackson spin. Ready? Here, that's no place to put a basement."

He has emptied dance floors from England to Spain. But as long as you granted my dad some floor space (by dancing in another club), he was essentially harmless. Rather like bar-top dancing in Singapore. Well, at least I think so and I have the support of Prime Minister Goh Chok Tong on this one.

Speaking on National Day 2002, the PM suggested that Singapore might allow bar-top dancing. It doesn't at the moment.

According to the Public Entertainment Act, dancing has to be confined to a dance floor that is "demarcated by permanent fixtures at least one metre high."

Er, *what?*

Never mind the Dutch coverage needed to get up and bar-dance, I'd need a few beers to understand the law preventing it. What I want to know is, who are the people who waste trees to write this rubbish on paper? Have they been to a club before? Have they conversed with women before?

I'd love to see them chat up women with a line like: "Excuse me, madam, but you have a lovely pair of 'permanent fixtures'." But it seems that bar-top dancing, as seen in the American movie *Coyote Ugly*, is a really, really serious issue for some Singaporeans. The subject was a topic for discussion on a Mediacorp TV talk show I watched one evening and I noticed that two phrases kept popping up — "Asian values" and "good monitoring".

I respect and admire genuine Asian values, with their emphasis upon the family unit and filial piety, but on this occasion they are being used as an excuse, not a reason. It reminds me of newspaper headlines like: "Maid Abused For Not Giving Wealthy *Tai Tai* Face" ('It was Asian values, Your Honour').

On the talk show, I heard someone say: "We grow up with Asian values, which means we are not prepared for those evil Westerners who corrupt us with pretty, scantily clad girls dancing on bars. These dancers will poison the young, insult the aunties, arouse the uncles, bring down the parliamentary system, cause anarchy in the streets, intensify the haze and global warming and force a passing meteorite to hit Mohammed Sultan Road in 2010."

Or words to that effect anyway. Besides, anyone who uses the term 'scantily clad' deserves our attention at all times — preferably through the window of a padded cell.

Then there was the idea of 'good monitoring'. There must be 'good monitoring' to protect the perilous dancers as they perform their death-defying routines. Some suggested protective clothing and iron bars. But that's not going to guarantee the young ladies' safety, is it? So, I'm offering a solution — The Mummy Bar-Top Dance. Realising that some Singaporeans like fads (Hello Kitty, bubble tea, sushi bars and Manchester United), I came up with a new one.

Bar owners should swathe their dancers from head to toe in protective bandages. Wellington boots should also be thrown in to prevent slipping, while sunglasses can reduce the glare from strobe lights. The dancers can then get into a glass cage, which is assembled at a safe distance from the crowd — 50 metres should be sufficient. Bouncers who would make Mike Tyson look like Mini-Me from *Austin Powers* will protect the cage.

Cushions can then be placed around the bar. Remember, these bars can reach astonishing heights — some are even rumoured to be one metre high. And as a final, safety measure, an ambulance, a doctor, two stretcher-bearers and a full medical crew will be on standby.

There is still a fear, however, that such erotic mummy dancing could arouse male drinkers. So, they can be hosed down with ice-cold water at 30-minute intervals, thus ensuring that the only things in the bar that remain erect are those 'permanent fixtures'. This is, of course, ridiculous. Yet, the rest of the world is watching this on-going farce.

Remember, foreigners are not interested in tedious facts about low crime rates and high living standards, they are interested in stereotypes, which are much more fun. And this bar-top nonsense has added another bullet to the gun.

Having just returned from Australia, I had to endure all the usual jokes. In Alice Springs, I was asked: "You're from Singapore? Don't they cut your hands off for chewing gum?"

"No," I replied, giving my stock answer. "That's for littering. Chewing gum warrants decapitation. After which, your head is stuck on a spike in Orchard Road to deter future gum-chewers."

It's most annoying and this dancing debate is adding fuel to the fire. So if bars like Coyote Ugly want to introduce the American dance craze to boost revenue, then why not? In this recession, I'd rather watch beautiful girls performing well-rehearsed routines, than sit in an empty bar with all the atmosphere of a mortuary.

God knows I've been to enough Singaporean bars where I've had to suffer deeply boring men screaming into handphones. On one or two occasions, I've even been to nightclubs and watched executives tapping away at their laptops. Other than using a hammer and a chisel to knock their computers up their back passage, I really don't know what you're supposed to do with these people. Give me a sexy, well-paid dancer over a kiasu ugly man every time.

So let's make it happen, preferably without the mummy costumes, but hey, whatever brings in the customers. If it doesn't, them I'm tempted to unleash a far more dangerous dance routine upon Singapore — my drunken father doing the moonwalk.

NOTE: I've since been to Coyote Ugly, for purely research purposes, of course, and I was delighted to see the dancers up on the bars and having a few laughs. Unsurprisingly, the heavens didn't fall, the seas haven't risen and the bar hasn't been struck by an evil plague of locusts. But the place is doing tremendous business. I can't think why.

THE TRIP

HAVING just returned from a weekend in the Indonesian island of Batam, I was reminded of two absolute certainties in life.

First, I always live up to my *ang moh* billing and bring back a face redder than a blushing lobster. I only have to poke my head out of the shade momentarily and the Indonesian sun will insist on giving me a souvenir. For the rest of the weekend, the hotel chef fries his eggs on my forehead.

Secondly, and more importantly, the *kiasu* brigade always decides to spend a loud weekend with me. It's got to the point where the travel agent asks "When would you like to travel?" and I reply, "I'll go with the *kiasus* because I'm emotionally imbalanced and my psychiatrist needs the income."

These Batam trips have already put me in a psychological conundrum as a result of the recent national stayer-quitter emigration debate. Within 24 hours of returning, I was on the psychiatrist's couch asking: "Does it really make me a bad person? I mean, I think I'm a stayer. But when I go to Batam for the weekend, I rarely, if ever, have nostalgic pangs for Singapore. I don't think about chicken rice, Orchard Road, one-party governments or anything. Does this make me a quitter? Because when I'm here, and no one is around, I do have guilty, longing thoughts for Batam. What do you think?"

"I think... Oh dear, time's up. That'll be 50 dollars. And, I must say, have you seen the state of your sunburn?"

Incidentally, if I ever mention the riveting stayer-quitter debate again, you may take a red-hot poker and thrust it repeatedly in my groin. Such a course of action is also useful when dealing with the *kiasu* brigade.

Unlike secret societies, *kiasu* members reveal themselves early, usually at Batam's ferry terminal. It's only been 45 minutes since we left Singapore, but they just couldn't wait to spring into action. Indonesian Immigration officers who, rather mischievously, open only two counters are partially to blame. When the queues are long enough, they open a third counter and announce: "On your marks, get set... *kiasu*."

One chap, carrying a bag full of golf clubs, *sprinted* from one queue to another — covering a distance of 10 metres in 1.5 seconds. His wife, who had been holding the hands of her two unsuspecting children, followed just behind. For several seconds, the children were airborne. By the time the breathless mother had caught up, her two offspring had completed two cartwheels, a double-back somersault and had contemplated a career in acrobatics.

My vision blurred after that. There were vague images of aunties running, luggage trolleys trundling over my toes, shopping bags scratching my legs and someone losing their patience and poking a runner in the eye. Though, on reflection, that could have been me. Then, miraculously, the dust settled and a third queue had formed.

And then it occurred to me. The *kiasus* should be head-hunted by the Singapore Sports Council. The Olympic 100 metres final would be a formality, if certain apparatus were permitted. Line up the *kiasus* against the finest American sprinters and set them off. After 50 metres or so, wheel out an immigration counter and place it at the end of their track lane. It wouldn't even be a contest.

For eager *kiasu*-watchers, though, ferry terminals certainly have a high strike rate. At the Singapore arrival hall, there was a delay at the security checkpoint thanks to — potato chips. A traveller had brought back enough bags to feed Toa Payoh. The snacks only cost 20 cents in Singapore, so after spending 40 dollars on his ferry ticket, how much money is he saving? Does he know something we don't? Are we on the threshold of a global potato-chip famine? If so, then this man stands to make, well, 20 cents a packet.

The Batam tourism board must be informed. It should come up with a new slogan — forget the golf, come for the potato chips. Currently, the island is sold as a rural haven — 45 minutes from Singapore, with rainforests, a warm climate and a fine cultural heritage. In Singlish, this is translated as: "Cheap *makan*, seafood also can. Cheap golf, cheap hotels, cheap shopping, fake branded goods also can. Cheap VCDs, illegal one also can. Pay Singapore dollars? Also can."

In fact, at my hotel, a Singaporean couple complained because they only had Singaporean dollars and they had calculated that the item they wanted cost less in Indonesian rupiah. Now, where's that red-hot poker when you need it?

As for me, I visit the island periodically because I'd heard Batam is a popular place for Singaporeans to keep a mistress.

And when you're a foreigner, you must try to fit in and adopt the local customs.

I caught a rather beautiful Indonesian waitress looking at me so I flashed my Toa Payoh library card (it looks like a credit card if you do it quickly) to win her over. It worked. She came over, looked into my eyes and said: "Have you seen the state of your sunburn?"

NOTE: I still go to Batam regularly. I still get sunburnt.

THE DRIVE

I CAN'T drive. No, that's not quite true. I can drive, I just can't pass the test. For some reason, driving instructors and examiners have always lost faith in me for minor lapses of concentration, which have resulted in knocking off another car's bumper during a three-point turn, mounting a kerb and narrowly missing a parked car and almost causing a 15-car pile-up at a gargantuan roundabout known as Gallows Corner in Essex. I'm not making any of that up. My sublime driving prowess is hereditary. My mother never passed her test either because she has a penchant for driving into ditches. It's a rare skill. I've spent many a childhood summer climbing out of a vertically parked car to enjoy the sunshine.

For some reason, my mother favoured country lanes because they were low on traffic. Unfortunately, they were high on roadside ditches. As we approached a bend, cries of "Mind that ditch" were always followed with "What ditch?"

"That fucking ditch! The one we are now sitting in. Sideways."

Until recently, I believed it was a curse against my family.

But finally, my sister broke the spell by passing her driving test. She's up there with Michael Schumacher as far as I'm concerned. After demonstrating remarkable reflexes to avoid that roundabout pile-up, my driving instructor turned to me and said: "I just don't know what to do with you anymore. You've reached the stage where you've actually become a danger to yourself and the other drivers around you. What happened at the roundabout... Well, I'm still shaking. It was just luck that stopped us from crashing. I've never seen anything like that."

In my defence, though, he'd never driven in Singapore. In England, when you drive as recklessly as I did, you fail every time. In Singapore, such behaviour appears to be rewarded with a Mercedes Benz and a free handphone. Now I know that criticism of Singaporean drivers has almost become a cliché in itself. I had never commented upon it before because we'd never had any direct experiences to draw upon.

Then, a week before Chinese New Year, we decided to hire a car. Despite having the mental age of a slightly backward four-year-old, my girlfriend is remarkably competent behind the wheel. We were toying with the idea of having a mini-driving holiday over the New Year period, with a drive up to Mount Ophir in Johor, Malaysia, which I'm told is a peach of a place with wild environments and animals aplenty. But the missus had never driven in Singapore before so we decided to spend the weekend burning rubber along the expressways. I mean tyre rubber, not the rubber they burn in parked cars up Mount Faber. She'd driven all over the south of England, Western Australia and along dirt roads in the Northern Territory's Outback. Singapore should be a breeze — like a drive in the country (with no ditches), right?

We witnessed two accidents in two days. My girlfriend has driven for over 10 years now and had never seen a crash while driving before. And in two days in Singapore, we saw two. What does that tell you? Admittedly, we were on the roads for at least eight hours each day but still the odds must be outlandish. The first incident was comparatively minor. At the busy junction off Bugis, a taxi clipped another car as they both turned right. Aside from a little broken glass and a crumpled wing, there was little to see. But that didn't stop the traffic crawling along so *kaypoh* drivers could gawk at the taxi driver and the woman who was in the other car. It also gave me a chance to criticise women drivers. Yes, I will take every opportunity to bolster my suspect masculinity.

The second crash, though, was more serious. Sitting at the traffic lights beside Lower Seletar Reservoir, my missus shouted: "Neil, he's going to fall off." There was a motorcycle turning right into the other side of the road, but he took the corner too sharply. Carrying a heavy load on the back of the bike didn't help and he toppled off, sliding along the fast lane for a couple of seconds. He actually stopped only a few feet from our car. But we were separated by the central reservation divider. The guy was obviously in some distress. Then, we saw the sort of thing that only fuels my misanthropic tendencies. The kind of incident which makes you think that an apocalypse might not be the end of the world.

The traffic lights changed so cars from the other side of the road moved across the junction and towards the stricken motorcyclist. They slowed, I assumed, to enable someone to get out and help him. But they didn't. They slowed to overtake him. That's right. As the injured man lay on the floor clutching his bleeding leg, cars pulled out and around him. They paused briefly, of course, to stare at the poor chap, and then they drove off. At least half a dozen cars did this. It's highly unlikely that such people will ever read this book. They're usually devoid of a sense of humour and spend their free time either boring listeners about property prices or battering maids. When they're not overtaking crash victims, of course. But should one or two of them pick up this book, having incorrectly assumed they can grow rich with it, then may I humbly say: You are a disgrace to humanity. If you could drive to the top of Mount Faber and then kindly jump off it, then there'd be one less *kiasu* prick for Singaporean society to worry about. Consider it your civic duty.

I'm sure you're not surprised that such parasites still live among us. A few years ago, I was on my way back to the office when my colleague and I saw a motorcyclist slam into a taxi. We quickly stopped and ran across to help. It was one of the worst injuries I have ever seen. The screaming motorist's foot was hanging off at the ankle. Moreover, the bones around his foot and ankle had been broken and twisted so severely that his foot pointed inwards, effectively in the opposite direction. I phoned the office to let the guys know I was going to be a bit late because we were going to wait for the ambulance and I was reprimanded. I was ordered to get back to the office immediately. When I returned, I suggested the decision was a bit harsh so I suffered the standard lecture about "my priorities and how the company should always be at the top of the list".

In Singapore's corporate world, you hear this hackneyed bullshit quite often in the office environment, don't you? Whenever I hear the sentence, "Well Neil, you must question your priorities," I stifle a yawn and head for the classified section.

I no longer work for that company. My general rule of thumb has always been: 'Unless you're a hooker, avoid working under too many arseholes.'

At the junction off Lower Seletar Reservoir, I was beginning to think the drivers on the other side of the road were all heading for a 'We're All Arseholes And We Love It!' convention. Eventually, and I'm really not making this up, a Mercedes attempted to drive around the victim's motorbike, but the car was too wide, jutting out dangerously into the next lane. So the driver pulled back and got out of the car to help him. Then others joined her. They had no choice, did they? Her Mercedes was blocking their path completely now. I went across the divider to help just as the lights changed, which meant my missus had no option but to pull away, do a U-turn into the side of the road where the bike crash was and drive off into the opposite direction because there was nowhere to stop. When she tried to slow down, she was beeped by other cars behind. I tried to beep back at them, but they couldn't hear me and I was busy trying to get the bike off the road with the help of a couple of taxi drivers. In the end, the missus got lost, drove a couple of kilometres in the wrong direction before completing one giant loop to come back and get me. By then, the motorcyclist was sitting on the grass verge speaking to his boss on his handphone, his bike had been moved and most of the debris had been cleared and I was roasting in the midday sun. By the time Mrs. Schumacher returned from her jaunty tour of Lower Seletar, I was ready to throw the daft cow into the reservoir.

We never drove to Malaysia for Chinese New Year in the end. There was no guarantee that I wouldn't end up in a police cell, charged with extreme road rage. On three separate occasions, the missus pulled me back into the car as I attempted to play 'Hide the Gearstick up the Rectum' with other drivers. I'm not sure what the offending drivers must have thought when they saw a lanky *ang moh* jump out of the car shouting: "Right, that's it, you *kiasu* fucker. That's one overtaking too many, you impatient bastard. Hang on, my minuscule missus is pulling me back into the car. But if she wasn't here..."

There are two prerequisites required to being accepted in the Singaporean driving community. Firstly, you must overtake continuously. In any lane. At any time. A bird's eye view of any major road in Singapore would just be a blur of zigzagging vehicles, gliding past each other like some well-choreographed dance routine. I'm sure it's necessary because the Republic is such a vast country, isn't it? If you were travelling from, say, Toa Payoh to Junction 8 at Bishan, the zigzagging manouevre must shave whole seconds off your driving time.

And don't forget to horn! Many drivers, particularly cabbies, seem to grab their horn and show it off to the world more frequently than a porn star. My particular favourite is when you are sitting in a mini-traffic jam waiting for the lights to change. Even though you could be six or seven cars down the line, the second the lights turn green up ahead, if you haven't revved your engine, you will get another man's horn. Now, you may call me old-fashioned in the modern age of sexual liberalism, but I've never wanted to receive another man's horn. You should savour it, gentlemen, only using it on special occasions. Otherwise it will become predictable and ordinary and it will lose its rarity value. Besides, if you waste your horn on me in a traffic jam, I will inevitably retort: "There are six cars in front of me. Where the fuck would you like me to go? You prick."

But that's just me. Or so I thought. In early 2003, there was a high-profile case of road rage in Singapore. A prominent expatriate businessman, from England, lost his temper with a taxi driver and punched him. Well, that's what the judge eventually concluded, based upon the cabbie's facial injuries. According to the expat twat, he merely "brushed the cabbie aside" during their little skirmish. The bruises on the cab driver's face suggested he'd been brushed aside with a hammer. As I'm sure you've discovered by now, there are expatriates in Singapore who are masterful bullshitters, borderline con men, really. They are capable of some absolute whoppers if it helps them get a highly paid job, keep a highly paid job or get a reduced jail sentence.

It reminds me of another mini-court case that involved a car crime. At my university hall of residence, a guy on my corridor got drunk one night and stole a radio from an unlocked car. The hall held an impromptu kangaroo court to determine whether or not the idiot should be kicked out. When asked how he came to be in the possession of another man's radio, the idiot replied: "Well sir, I'd had a few drinks and things were a bit hazy. It was foggy that night so visibility was a bit poor. Then, I looked down, and suddenly I was holding a car radio. To this day, I have no idea how it got there." He was booted out of the hall and screwed up his university degree. It wouldn't surprise me if he was a CEO in a Singaporean company now — still lying his arse off.

But for the guy who can smash in people's faces with a mere brush-off, bullshit would not save him in Singapore this time. The driving savage was sentenced to four months — a ridiculously small sentence. I can't see a Singaporean being treated so leniently, can you?

But his case both alarmed and shamed me. On three occasions, I was only one step away from losing my rationality. Perhaps all aggressive drivers or passengers should drive with my missus. For many years now, Singapore has spoilt many Caucasians by providing them with lucrative salary packages, condominiums and, quite often, an undeserved cultural pedestal to stand on. It would be disgraceful if expatriates, particularly British, reciprocated by promoting two of their biggest social successes — a drinking culture and road rage.

But, ironically, Singaporean drivers have gone to the opposite extreme. There is a kind of laissez faire apathy on the roads. Other drivers overtake on the inside line, narrowly missing your vehicle, so you have no choice but to do likewise, right? Other idiots like to sound their horn at traffic lights, so the sheep follow the shepherd and the intolerance and impatience endures.

I asked my old mate Dave, a Singaporean and a bloody good driver, how this selfish, reckless driving culture evolved. He told me: "In Singapore, it's just the way it is now. If you don't do it, you won't get to work on time. You will be late. So if you don't cut in and pull out on another car, you'll be stuck there waiting to turn left all day. Because no one else will let you out. That's how it is. Everybody does it."

That's how it is. The apathy endures. Everybody does it, so what choice does the average Singaporean driver have? I disagreed with Dave. There are one or two Singaporeans who batter their maids and leave their so-called children in 24-hour daycare centres, but that doesn't mean I must follow suit. Though I am more than willing to employ these bastards as road obstacles the next time I take my driving test.

But this nationwide apathy is like a disease permeating through society and it threatens to rip out the soul and break the backbone of one of the greatest countries I've ever known. To me, it seems top-down. In a one-party state, you have no alternative in the political sphere. You have no alternative in the economic sphere, with this never-ending recession. You have no alternative in the social sphere, because if you emigrate you will be labelled a "quitter" so don't even think about trying to come back. And now, it seems, you don't even have an alternative behind a bloody steering wheel. This mindset has taken Darwinism to its most extreme and boring form.

However, that is nothing compared to the 'Mercedes culture'. Where in the name of social snobbery did that come from? I was out with a friend once and a Mercedes cut right across our car, missing the left wing by a few inches. Pulling down the window, I was about to offer my compliments for an outstanding manouevre which almost maimed me when my friend pulled me back.

"Don't say anything to him," he warned.

"Why not?"

"That's an expensive car he's got there. Probably a big-shot CEO or something. Better not say anything." Do the words 'bull', 'red' and 'rag' mean anything to you? They did to me and I was even more determined to shout at somebody.

"You're telling me I've got to allow this prick to drive recklessly because he has a bigger bank account than us?"

"It's not that," my friend explained carefully. "Singapore is a tiny place, especially in business. The chances of you running into this guy at a meeting or in the office are quite high. If you don't give him face, he could remember it and screw your career."

"Yeah? I'd never thought of it. Well, in that case, fuck him."

This Singaporean symbiotic relationship between material wealth and social status has got to be broken up. Money does not equate to courtesy. It might be just me here, but have you noticed that some of the biggest arseholes — the most self-centred, selfish, tedious, dogmatic individuals — that Singapore can offer are often *towkays*? Rich, miserable old bastards who assume they can bypass you at the queue in the garage and force you to brake sharply on the expressway so their luxury vehicle can smoothly dominate whichever lane it chooses.

Just a few weeks ago, I was standing in the middle of a junction at Toa Payoh Central, waiting for the lights to change, when I watched some moronic *tai tai* attempt a U-turn in her Mercedes. There's nothing illegal or inconsiderate about that. However, she tried to turn the wheel of her huge car with her right hand, while she held her handphone with her left. In the middle of her earpiece-free conversation, it was painfully obvious that her minuscule powers of concentration were being stretched to their limit. She turned so slowly that oncoming cars were forced to slow down as she straddled two lanes, forcing other cars to swerve away from a huge insurance bill. But she was oblivious to all of this, of course. Without so much as a casual glance in her rear-view mirror, the silly bitch continued her conversation and pulled away.

These buggers do not own the road. And I'm going to be brutally honest here. I've been in a car with my face-giving friend on several occasions and listened to him savage other drivers. He says things like: "You see that bastard there overtake me? Look at his number plate. He's a Malaysian, what do you expect?

Buggers can't even drive properly." Or "Look at that shitty car there. A cheap Nissan and he thinks he can drive around like a big shot." He is the same person who says things like: "Never mind *lah*. Did you see his BMW? That's the new model, *shiok* right? Costs about 150k, that model."

By the time he's finished arse-kissing the vehicle's owner, he's forgotten that it was only his quick reflexes that prevented the '*shiok* new model' from knocking his wing mirror off.

So it's time for the Singaporean government to step in and ban inconsiderate *towkays* and *tai tais* from ever driving a car in this city-state again. Should one or two of the more liberal members of this society consider such a stipulation a tad harsh, then I recommend employing chauffeurs. Such distinguished citizens should have no problem paying for a personal driver. Now, I've spoken to my mother and she's more than willing to do the job. We've just got to find the deepest ditch in Singapore.

THE SNIP

LIKE many movie distributors in Singapore, I've also been punished for trying to show uncensored films.

When I was a child, my younger sister and I would raid the video cabinet as soon as our mother left for work in a bid to find the juiciest material. We succeeded but, unfortunately, our movie selections were always discovered. Our mother would return and notice that two videotapes — *The Violent Return of the Sick, Sordid, Sadistic Serial Killer* and *The Sound of Music* — had not been rewound.

"How many times have I told you? You must stop your little sister from watching violent films," our mother would shout.

"Sorry, mum. I was too busy watching Julie Andrews in my bedroom. I'm sorry."

"Sorry?!" she would scream. "That's not good enough. Sorry? I'll give you 'sorry'."

She did not give me a 'sorry', whatever that was. Instead, she gave me a forceful slap on the face that sent me over the sofa like an Olympic hurdler. I've been opposed to all forms of artistic censorship ever since.

Over the years, though, I've managed to block out my mother's random acts of violence. But the memories came flooding back when video censorship sneaked into the news again.

A report in *TODAY* said that those guys down at the Films and Publications Department (FPD) had cut the outstanding *Gosford Park* DVD before it was sent out to the stores. Apparently, the British social satire showed a man's buttocks during its cinematic release, which was R(A)-rated, earlier in the year.

Now, call me old-fashioned, but I don't go to cinemas to ogle men's bums. If I wanted to look at a hairy, greasy and slightly flabby backside, I could stand on a mirror. So I can't even recall the two-second scene, but nothing gets past those eager beavers on the Films Advisory Panel who help to decide a movie's classification in Singapore.

They cut the scene for the DVD release, which has, in turn, thoroughly ruined the director's audio commentary. Nevertheless, we can all sleep safely in our beds now because there is one less bare bum out there. If that monu-mental decision doesn't single-handedly revive Singapore's flagging economy, then, frankly, nothing will.

And don't underestimate the workload of the FPD. After visiting its fascinating website, I learned that of the 39 movies reviewed from August 10 to September 9 in 2002, seven were passed only after cuts were made.

Some, of course, do not make it to the Republic's cinema screens at all. In February 2002, Ben Stiller's satire on the modelling industry, *Zoolander*, was denied a cinematic release. The silly, comical plot involved assassinating a mythical Malaysian president and was deemed insensitive.

Taking this issue into serious consideration, it might be an opportune time to reexamine the *James Bond* series. After all, there are several plots involving megalomaniacs seeking world domination, often at the expense of global superpowers. They might only be the work of fiction, but does the rest of the world know that? Downing Street and the White House must be informed.

But seriously, the *Gosford Park* farce hardly comes as a surprise. I've been a victim of the excitable, but clumsy, cutters at the FPD. A friend sent a British gangster movie to me, as a gift, and it was rerouted to those wonderful FPD employees.

Confident the film would escape the censors scissors, I paid for it to be viewed by those wonderful FPD employees, who decide, on my behalf, what parts of my gift I'm allowed to take home. However, I was staggered to learn that the movie was awarded two cuts, which I also had to pay for. One of the cuts involved a pair of exposed breasts *on a poster, in the background and out of focus*. Now, I'm quite partial to that area of a woman's body, but I must confess that I'd never even noticed the poster. But, thankfully, those wonderful FPD employees certainly did.

Are we supposed to deny the existence of breasts? Because, with the exception of Pamela Anderson's, they're real, you know. And there isn't a man (or woman, for that matter) who should not give thanks to their respective gods every single day. A slightly different chink in the evolutionary chain and breasts could have been shaped like cows' udders, which would've been a genuine reason to cut them completely from the movie-making process.

But interestingly, certain productions fall under the FPD's exempted categories. Examples include sports programmes, training videos, karaoke tapes and ballet recordings.

Has anyone at the FPD ever watched ballet on television? Those lycra numbers leave absolutely nothing to the imagination. It only takes a close-up, frontal shot of a male dancer pirouetting and I can't look at a chicken rice stall for a week. There are all sorts of things wiggling about in that costume. A performance of *Swan Lake* has more perfectly toned torsos than 20 viewings of an uncensored *Gosford Park*. For the sake of social cohesion and chicken rice stall owners everywhere, it is time for the FPD to take its scissors along to the ballet.

Certainly, some of these neurotic censors need to get out more and get a life. If that doesn't work, they can always get a gentle slap from my ever-willing mother.

NOTE: Within three days, I received a wonderful page-long letter from the FPD, which was subsequently published in the letters page of *TODAY*. The government body never took me to task for any of the content. It couldn't. It was all based on facts or actual incidents. But the censorship body felt the need to explain why the scissors came out for movies like *Gosford Park* — so it could receive a general certificate. In other words, making the cut means more copies of the DVD can be sold to a wider audience. I must admit I was quite impressed with FPD's reply, because it showed that the guys there just had a job to do and they all took the column in the right spirit. But it remains disappointing that in the interests of making a few extra dollars, art continues to come off second best to greed in Singapore.

THE PHANTOM

MY senile grandmother doesn't understand the concept of recycling. Environmental issues mean nothing to her. She can't even spell 'environment'. She endured London's pea-soup smog of the '50s, when levels of sulphur reached lethal concentrations with no fuss and typical working-class resilience. Indeed, if she visited Singapore, she would consider the haze a 'slightly overcast' day.

I asked her once what she thought about recycling and she said: "If your granddad was still alive, you could've asked him. He was never off that bloody bike."

Like many of the aunties and uncles in Singapore, she has little time for recycling. But for a country that could easily fit into several Canadian lakes, wastage is like a foul odour that won't go away. Recently, a number of environmentally conscious Singaporeans have complained about the lack of awareness regarding the various laudable recycling programmes that have existed for some time.

The Ministry of Environment, which has, in truth, made commendable efforts to minimise the waste of some four million people, should send a team down to Toa Payoh. Tucked away in an HDB block is the phantom recycler, a potential environmental envoy for the country who could keep the country green for your grandchildren. I discovered him when I moved house. Yes, it was time to call it a day on Toa Payoh Lorong 1. We had some good times, but we decided to part ways to maintain an amicable relationship.

I moved from Lorong 1 all the way to… Lorong 2. You didn't seriously think I was going to turn my back on Toa Payoh, did you? If I go any further north than Bishan, I start to get a nosebleed.

It was a rather bizarre moving day anyway because the moving lady possessed the unique skill of conjuring rabbits. Apparently, someone on my old corridor had to get rid of a pair of rabbits because they were mating like, well, rabbits. They were producing the kind of numbers that Romancing Singapore campaigners can only dream of and all that 'producing', scratching and cries of "oh yeah, bunny boy" were keeping the old timer awake at night. So, he gave the rabbits to my removal lady. But she never told me.

Can you possibly imagine what your reaction would be if you unloaded your belongings off a lorry and discovered two randy rabbits that you know you didn't have 20 minutes ago? You would probably say: "Excuse me, auntie. Sorry to trouble you, but where the fuck did you get these shagging rabbits from?" Or something like that.

But that was only the first illusion during a weekend that quickly became a David Copperfield special. Like most people, we'd accumulated too much junk for a three-room flat. I'm still not sure why I have a life-sized Darth Vader mask, for instance, but there you go. First, we called in the Salvation Army. I wasn't aware that they'd moved into recycling. When I was a child, they just blew out a few Christmas carols on their trumpets and disappeared again until the following December. But they collected six bags of 'why-in-the-name-of-impulse-buying-did-you-buy-THAT-you-stupid-woman' stuff and promised to pass it on to the needy.

Then, we called in the collectors at SembCorp Waste Management to take the rest, that is, the sort of knick-knacks that the Salvation Army turned down, giving you an idea of the crap my girlfriend had accumulated. But no disrespect to either recycling programme; nothing compares to the resourcefulness of the phantom recycler of Toa Payoh.

In a rare moment of recklessness, I'd bought a junior snooker table once, swearing that it would have to be prised from my dead hands before I'd get rid of it. The missus threatened to leave me if she bumped into the green beast one more time on her way to the toilet in the dead of night. So I took it down to the HDB lift lobby to get rid of it. But, before that, I took a box down containing the snooker cues, the balls and so forth. When I returned less than five minutes later with the table, the box had vanished. There was no trace of it. Now, I suffer from a rancid imagination, but, without the table, what the hell does a person want with a pair of snooker cues and another man's balls? Frankly, I was genuinely stumped on that one.

I considered David Copperfield but quickly dismissed him. I know he made the Statue of Liberty disappear, but could he make his balls disappear outside an HDB lift in Toa Payoh? I was intrigued, so I staked out a nearby void deck and watched my snooker table for 10 minutes. Nothing happened. Bored and hungry, I went back upstairs to lock up and when I returned, the table had disappeared! Who the hell was doing this?

Growing alarmed, I grabbed a passer-by and said: "Hi, I've just moved into this block. I wonder if you can help me?" By his concerned reaction, I'm sure he visualised all-night parties, too much beer, English Premiership matches blaring out at 4am and drunken brawls between rival supporters. But he shouldn't feel compelled to invite me over. So I hurriedly continued: "Have you seen a snooker table outside the lift?"

"What's it look like?"

"A washing machine."

"Really?"

"No. It's big, green, rectangular, with pockets in every corner."

"No, I haven't. But I know someone who can get the new Incredible Hulk movie on DVD if you're interested?"

I wasn't. But I am keen for the environment ministry to employ the phantom to improve its recycling statistics. In 2000, Singapore generated 4.6 million tonnes of waste and recycled 1.8 million tonnes of them, giving a recycling rate of 40 per cent. In 2001, that level increased to 2.2 million tonnes from 5 million tonnes of waste. Thus, the recycling rate increased to a commendable 44 per cent. And it's trying to raise residential awareness with the National Recycling Programme (NRP), which was launched in April 2001. If you're interested, household participation began at around 15 per cent. It reached 30 per cent by October last year. The NRP is aiming for a 50 per cent participation rate by the end of 2003, and I sincerely hope it succeeds. I don't want to leave a

Singaporean rubbish dump for your grandchildren, do you?

But I'm convinced that even the optimistic target of 50 per cent would be a conservative estimate if the environment ministry recruited the phantom recycler of Toa Payoh. Get the Internal Security Department to hold stakeouts at the HDB blocks in Toa Payoh Lorong 2. The agents must scour the void decks to find this man immediately. He will clean up this country before you can say: "Have you seen my bloody snooker table?"

THE FARECARD

THE peaceful tranquillity of Malaysia's Tioman Island was shattered, when my partner grabbed my arm and exclaimed: "We need to get an ez-link card!"

I had no idea what the stupid woman was talking about either. Sitting at the jetty waiting for a ferry, this was hardly the place to be discussing the Singaporean public transport system. We had spent a rustic weekend at a simple village, where the locals were so laidback they were almost horizontal. When the ferry was 10 minutes late, I asked the operator: "What time is the ferry due?"

"When it gets here," came the humbling reply. "Don't worry, sit back, relax and feed the fish."

Great advice, but I didn't have any bread and, besides, we had to rush back to Singapore, apparently, to embark on our ez-link card mission. An eager bus driver had informed me the previous week that the prehistoric farecard was to be bumped off on October 1, 2002, and that we risked social castration if we didn't have an ez-link card by then. So, from the serene silence of Tioman, we joined the shuffling feet at Toa Payoh's MRT station. The queue for the ticket booth was longer than the Great Wall of China. What were they all queuing for? I'm convinced that some had no idea.

"Look at that!" Passers-by must say to their friends. "Now that's what I call a queue. Sure must be a free gift at the end. Come *lah*."

In the end, though, I was granted a temporary reprieve. After calling a charming woman on the TransitLink hotline, I discovered that the death of the farecard would be a long, drawn out process. She said it could be "November or even December" before the ez-link card usurps its predecessor and takes complete control. That being the case, I will doggedly persevere with the old farecard until Dec 31.

And I know this will irritate fellow commuters. On buses, when I slow down boarding time with my farecard fumbling, the perverse side of me quite enjoys the accompanied critical mutterings. If they persist, I turn the card upside down, look aghast when the machine spits it back and say: "Excuse me, there seems to be something wrong with the machine and I'm really in a hurry here." God, where do they get these people from?

But I struggle with relentless change. My generation has grown up in a society where Blitzkrieg technological development is the norm. There is no time to stand still. I admire those who stand up for some continuity in their lives.

In England, there were cases of shopkeepers being forced, by law, to adopt the metric system of weights and measures in line with European Union stipulations. Despite the threat of a fine, and in extreme cases a prison sentence, they still stuck by their pounds and ounces. They were my heroes.

These grocery guys would rather take on the European Union than risk the wrath of little old ladies coming in and asking: "What the bloody hell is a gram, you silly young man? Now, give me two pounds of sugar before I box your ears."

In some ways, this was a wise move because the only people that measured in grams when I last lived in England were drug dealers. And they're most welcome to them. So, I will continue on my crusade to preserve some traditions and hold back the technological tide for as long as possible. But it's difficult not to get trampled under the march towards greater efficiency.

According to the various transport operators in Singapore, the new ez-link card relies on the Global Positioning System (GPS) of satellites to track the location of the bus. So if you're reading this on a bus while picking your nose, then let me assure you that the GPS has you in its sights. Think about that. Now, go and wash your finger.

But when the ez-link card was first introduced, there were some glitches in the system with cards being misread or overcharged on buses and trains. So, in April 2002, a Bus Task Force was established to remove the kinks and increase ez-link's efficiency.

Yes, that's a Bus Task Force — in proud capital letters, no less. I assume this means that muscle-bound men in ski masks, abseil from helicopters onto the roofs of buses and shoot, on sight, anyone whose ez-link card is rejected by the reader. Machine-gunning their way through the bus, the fearsome task forcers will cry: "Right, you dithering bastards, the next person to slow down this bus by pissing about with their ez-link card will get a bullet in the balls. Oh, sorry, I didn't realise this was a school bus."

If that doesn't speed up boarding time, nothing will. No, wait, perhaps they should introduce those moving floors that they have at airports. You could just step on and have your ez-link card scanned as you glide past. If the machine fails to read the card, rather than emit that repetitive beep, it should administer an electric shock. Watch how fast the commuters move down the aisle then.

Don't laugh; there's probably a civil servant involved with public transport reading this and thinking: "Actually, an electric shock device could speed up boarding time by 0.3 seconds. That would make each bus route 4.7 seconds faster. And that, most importantly of all, could add 0.8 per cent to my increment at the end of the year."

It could happen. And when the Bus Task Force starts landing on my bus in Thomson Road, I'll head for Tioman. You'll find me lying in a hammock, fanning myself with my old farecard.

NOTE: True to form, I continued with my trusty farecard until December 2002, when I returned to England for a working holiday. When I came back in the new year, I went straight on the bus and tried to use my farecard. My fellow passengers looked at me as if I had just shit on the floor. I had to use cash in the end. But to this day, I still forget to swipe the ez-link card as I leave the bus. So, if you spot a sweaty *ang moh* running back towards the bus eloquently shouting, "Wait, you bastard, I forgot to beep this fucking stupid card", please refrain from calling the police again.

THE SKIN

EVEN though it was my friend's birthday, I didn't want to go to a nightclub. I no longer drink and when I try to dance soberly, the crowd parts frantically and someone usually makes a desperate call to the Singapore Zoo to discuss my recapture.

"But it's your boss' birthday," my colleagues pleaded.

"I've never even heard of the club," I retorted.

"It's off Orchard Road. The area's also known affectionately as 'the four floors of whores'."

"I see. What time are we leaving?"

Once I'd handed over a month's salary in exchange for an entry stamp and a tepid Coke, it became immediately obvious that something was amiss. The clientele's diversity was staggering. There were over 50 white, expat males, which made up around 80 per cent of all the men in the club — and just two white women. Many of the men were older than my father. Some even danced like him, which was most disconcerting. I thought he was a one-off.

Just where do these people go during the day? If you stopped reading this book right now and walked 50 metres in any direction, I'll wager that you'll encounter very few *ang mohs*.

Step into any nightclub along Orchard Road at the weekend and you can't miss them. Like vampires, they prowl the dance floor looking for female victims and, my god, there was no shortage of eager sacrifices that night. I thought all this SPG nonsense was going the way of the expat CEO.

Have these young ladies not read the news? In recent months, *ang mohs* with fat wallets have been dropping like flies. Many are fleeing back to the West quicker than you can say: "You know, perhaps we should have hired that Nanyang guy after all. The New York guy nearly ruined us."

But no one, it seems, has relayed this information to the beguiling beauties currently doing the nightclub circuit. I've never encountered so many women harbouring obsessions with ageing 'foreign talents'.

There was only Ulrika Jonsson in England. The stunning TV presenter had a fling with the talented, though slightly unusual looking, Sven-Goran Eriksson. But Jonsson has had affairs with several sporting personalities, so it's difficult to deduce whether she actually had feelings for the England coach or just loved the smell of men's dressing rooms. Yet, even she would be out of her league in Orchard Road.

One gorgeous Malay girl, wearing a dress the size of a handkerchief, spent several hours flirting with no less than four different white men before settling for a plump, American chap. He couldn't believe his luck. She couldn't believe his wallet.

Clearly, there were just not enough *ang mohs* to go around. And this fact became painfully obvious when a tipsy 30-something made a beeline for me. Now, I'm not going to kid myself here. In England, women have remarked that, in a certain light, I resemble James Dean — albeit after his fatal car crash. I attract women like an Opposition candidate attracts votes in Toa Payoh. Yet this did not deter my new, distinctly exotic companion.

"Wha' your name?" she slurred.

"Stamford Raffles."

"Ha. Would you like me to dance with you?"

"Er, no. Thanks."

"Come lah, let me dance for you."

"With me or for me?"

"I dance for you."

"No, really. Thanks." Like the leaflet distributors, she just wouldn't bugger off.

"Don't be shy lah. Come, I sit on your lap."

"What?!" But it was too late. Before I could move, her backside came at me like a Tomahawk missile. My first reaction was to scream, my second to call for security and my third would've involved several sharp toothpicks. A quick shift to the left allowed me to narrowly escape her weighty plunge.

Yet, my physical rejection merely encouraged her. She stood up again, eager to launch herself a second time, so I dashed off to join my friend in the toilet. This desperate measure suggested that I was gay and she backed off, finally.

My poor friend at the urinal was besieged by questions. Who is that woman? Why does she want to gyrate on my groin? Where the hell did that long-stemmed red rose come from? And, most worryingly of all, where the bloody hell did she intend to put it? But that's it, as far as I'm concerned. The next time I go to a club, I'm wearing a sign — a huge placard across my chest that will say: "I NOT RICH, I NO CONDO, I LIVE IN HDB."

It's ironic, really, because in every other facet of Singaporean society, there is an increasing realisation that white skin does not automatically equate to a greater talent or bank balance. Except, of course, in the nightclubs — a situation that *ang mohs*, fat wallet or no fat wallet, are always keen to exploit.

But do not fear, because what goes around comes around. On the way home, I spotted a pair of middle-aged *ang mohs* chatting with two lanky ladies, while brandishing their wallets. As I approached, I noticed that the two women were, in fact, heavily made-up men — a biological fact that had gone unnoticed by the two drunks.

Now that's a truly novel way of introducing expats to the concept of value-added services. I just hope the two 'ladies' offered to show the *ang mohs* their long-stemmed red roses. But seriously ladies, it's time to stop putting *ang mohs* on a pedestal — or your lap.

NOTE: Unsurprisingly, quite a few letters came in over this controversial issue. But this time, interestingly, every one of them agreed with my rather critical views of exploitative Caucasians and naive Singaporeans. Many were just getting tired of the predictability of it all. So am I.

THE BAN

WHEN I was 18, I was banned from my local pub. Considering I grew up in a part of London where chicken molesting barely raised an eyebrow, this was quite an achievement. The public house was so dilapidated that when I first asked the barmaid where the toilet was, she replied: "You're in it."

On one hazy occasion, I found myself looking for the men's urinal in the ladies room. For some reason, the sight of women applying lipstick in the mirror didn't warrant concern. Probably because I was being strangled at the time by an irate landlord, who kept shouting obscenities like "pervert" and "dirty little bugger". Apparently, he was not impressed when I said I was looking for the jukebox. So, I was banned from one of the worst pubs in London.

Among friends, there was a certain cachet to being booted out of a notorious drinking den. The incident awarded me some priceless street-cred. It allowed me to concentrate on my A-Levels and gave me the opportunity to use the word 'cachet'.

But in Singapore, however, it is ridiculously easy to earn yourself a ban of any kind. Last year, a journalist was not allowed to attend functions of the Comfort Group, the taxicab company, after penning a critical commentary about its CEO and his supposedly generous salary package. This is grossly unfair.

I mean, where's the slap from incensed ladies whom you've embarrassed outside the toilet cubicle or the kick up the backside from bouncers? At the very least, a credible ban must be followed with a severe battering from your mother, preferably with a broom handle. It always did for me anyway. I mean, if bans are given out so cheaply, then why can't I have one and all the kudos that comes with it?

Attempting to answer this question, I met covertly with one of those 'disgruntled staff members' of the Comfort Group. There are plenty of them — they're called Singaporean taxi drivers. On the condition of anonymity, one cabbie told me everything. "Though must be careful, *ah*?" He cautioned. "Must protect my rice bowl. Unlike my bosses, my rice bowl very small. It's like my taxi — cannot smash."

He then proceeded to discuss the hypocrisy of big bosses at Comfort, the high rental of his vehicle and his astronomical insurance and petrol costs. It seemed too good to be true — this guy was revealing the complete inside story, a scoop no less, which would guarantee a ban and subsequent notoriety in media circles. It was too good to be true, however, because the driver was a raving lunatic. An utter fruitcake — his hands spent more time gesticulating than they did on the wheel. In fact, he treated the steering contraption like an electric fence and the more animated he became, the less he touched the wheel.

"Comfort threatened to sack me twice. You know why or not?" he bellowed.

"For not keeping your hands on the wheel, you bloody madman?" I offered.

"No, because I've had two accidents. They said I was a bad driver. Ridiculous right?" And then, he turned round to ascertain my reaction. That's right. We were careering along Thomson Road and the old loony turns around so I can reassure him that he is a competent driver. I wouldn't have trusted him with a shopping trolley.

"But what about your big boss?" I asked, pointing towards the windscreen, something he didn't acknowledge very often. "Was it fair of him to ban that journalist?"

The cabbie shrugged and said, "Singapore's like that. Even before your time, it's been like that."

Now, call me naive, but I thought those hip, swinging Singaporeans of wealth and power were dancing out of the shackles of stereotype. In a desperate bid to keep the younger ones from living with koala bears, kangaroos and crocodile hunter Steve Irwin, the Republic's elite is supposed to be more open and more tolerant of criticism. We're allowed to know the incomes of CEOs of public-listed companies, I'm told, because of something called 'corporate transparency'. But not everyone in the corporate world is ready to embrace this freewheeling, radical notion of transparency.

The Comfort Group proudly announced that the 'disgruntled staff member' who leaked news of the journalist's ban to the media has faced 'severe disciplinary action'. The employee was to be hanged, drawn and quartered, but the rack was still rusty after all that exertion during the Spanish Inquisition. So the guilty party settled for castration, followed by a quick, lethal injection.

This is just the kind of carefree, trusting environment that will convince the quitters to flood back to Changi Airport, isn't it?

Incidentally, if the bigwigs at Comfort ever feel like relocating to Australia, then my cabbie friend and I will gladly pay your airfare. I'll even get Mr. Look-No-Hands to drive you to the airport. Is that enough to earn me a ban now?

NOTE: Apparently, it was not enough to earn me a ban, which I was devastated about. I couldn't sleep for a fortnight afterwards. In media circles, I had to stand on the periphery and watch big-shot writers discuss their various establishment bans. It was so humiliating. However, having the article published in this book will certainly not do my chances any harm. So if you've bought this book, you have possibly contributed to a major transport operator banning me from ever being allowed to step into one of its taxicabs again. Nice one.

THE SEX

WELL, what a miserable month October, 2002, turned out to be for me and many other Singaporeans. Despite interviewing Oasis songwriter Noel Gallagher just the week before, the bad boys from Manchester proved to be no more than choirboys in the end. After the tragic Bali bombings, they decided that Singapore was not an oasis and returned to England with their guitars between their legs.

They had been due to play their first ever Singaporean gig at the Singapore Indoor Stadium, but the belligerent brothers shit themselves after a terrorist attack thousands of kilometres away. If there were similar nightclub bombings in Spain's Costa del Sol, would they cancel a gig in Britain? Besides, is Southeast Asia really that dangerous for Westerners? Surely the average British celebrity has more to fear from being cornered by British TV star and man-hunter Ulrika Jonsson at a showbiz party.

I'm a white man living in Singapore and the only bodily harm I fear is from being tapped to death by my mini-mart owner. Her palms pummel my forearms with every word she utters. And she does enjoy a sentence or two.

"Ah *ang moh*," she begins brightly, tapping my hand and arms. "More toilet rolls, is it? Too much curry again, is it?" Tap, tap, tap.

"You must watch your diet, eh?" Tap, tap, tap.

"Stop tapping me! I need all this tissue to wrap around my sore arms, you daft old bat."

I have left the shop with more bruises than a sadomasochist, which, incidentally, is my subtle way of introducing my next topic — sex. To be honest, it salvaged a miserable month as far as I was concerned. Rather depressed with the regional news, I was delighted to learn that, in some quarters, I'm considered to be obsessed with the physical act of lovemaking.

I received an email from a reader who said something like: "We've read your newspaper columns and come to the conclusion that you must be a pervert. Therefore we are promoting a number of board games designed to improve sexual relationships, and we thought of you."

Well, I was appalled, at first. And then I asked them to send me one of the games. Two days later, *FOREPLAY — A Game For Lovers* arrived on my desk.

It's like *Trivial Pursuit* for nymphomaniacs. You play the game with your wife or lover (or wife and lover, if you're feeling really bold) and, through a series of questions, you learn more about your partner's sexual desires, preferences and ambitions. The game finishes, hopefully, with you and your partner moving onto something a little more physically stimulating. No, not *Scrabble*. But you do get extra points for length.

The game is proving quite popular, I'm told, and can be bought by Singaporeans at *www.sensualfire.com.sg*.

But I remain skeptical. This is Singapore. In this country, you cannot even have SEX on a number plate — for several reasons. Firstly, the number plates aren't wide enough and you'd fall off and scratch your bare arse on the tarmac. Secondly, 'sex on a number plate' sounds like a song by Eminem. Thirdly, and perhaps most importantly, the Land Transport Authority recently decided against using vowels as the middle letter of three-letter prefixes in vehicle licence plates. Thus, sensitive words like SEX, SIN and SUX are avoided.

One *TODAY* letter writer applauded the decision, saying that her young son should not see his mother driving around in a car with the word SEX on it. How times have changed. When I grew up in Dagenham, which is on the outskirts of east London, children hoped to avoid seeing their mothers having sex *in* the car.

Considering that startling thought, is it fair to say that we are dealing with a more conservative society here? This is a country where a sex scene in Eminem's movie, *8 Mile*, has been cut even though both Eminem and his screen partner are *fully clothed* throughout their lovemaking session. The game's distributor, Passions Of Life, disagrees though, claiming that Asians invented the *Kama Sutra*, while Bangkok is the sex capital of the world, with Geylang, I believe, coming a close second.

This was the line I took with my girlfriend when I asked her to play *Foreplay* with me — all in the name of investigative journalism, of course. But the game didn't last long. One of the cards instructed her to sprinkle talcum powder on my neck. The dust irritated my sinuses, and I ended up looking and sounding like a pig with respiratory problems.

This irritated my girlfriend. I know because when I asked her, "Under what circumstances do you think the most enjoyable lovemaking sessions occur?" she replied, "When you're at work."

Rather miffed by her sarcasm, I asked two girls in the office to play the game together instead. This was a somewhat pitiful attempt on my part to realise a long-harboured fantasy involving two young ladies, preferably with bisexual tendencies and a steamy shower. Nothing of the sort happened. Though I was engrossed by the constant giggling and playful slapping, which was a trifle disturbing. In truth, though, it's just a bit of saucy fun and, God knows, we've needed some of that recently.

Without wishing to trivialise major global issues, I'd rather play *Foreplay* on a Saturday night than watch news of the latest gig cancellation, shooting or bombing. In fact, I fancy a game right now. Do you know Ulrika Jonsson's handphone number?

To be honest, though, I've got a better chance with the mini-mart auntie. No slap and tickle, just lots of bloody tapping.

NOTE: I was really pissed off when Oasis and a couple of other acts cancelled their Singaporean gigs after the Bali attacks last year. It demonstrated, once again, many Westerners' short-sighted and blinkered views of the region. If you read the British tabloids you could be forgiven for thinking: "All Muslims bad, all Asia Muslims, so all Asia bad."

On a personal level, Oasis has been my favourite band for years. I even managed to somehow mention the group in the introduction of my previous book, *Notes from an even Smaller Island*. So, as you can imagine, I was well chuffed when I got to interview Noel Gallagher, the creative force behind the band. Two days after the article was published, however, Oasis cancelled its gigs in both Singapore and the Philippines. I felt a right prick. Luckily for me, I had a new board game to cheer me up.

THE WHEEL

THE screaming was deafening. As the train pulled into the Canary Wharf station in east London, the pitiful high-pitched whine drew the attention of everyone on the carriage. It was most embarrassing because the panic-stricken voice was mine. We were going to crash! Demonstrating my characteristic strengths of Jonah, this was my first time on the state-of-the-art Docklands Light Railway and I end up with a driver who thinks he's Houdini. The bastard had disappeared.

"Look mum," I bellowed. "There's no driver. He's jumped out. We're going to smash into the station. We're all going to die."

My humiliated mother, as always, muttered something about "her stupid son showing her up in a public place" and silenced me with a subtle, but effective, slap across the face.

I should have maintained my cool. I should've known that the new transport system was automated and required no driver. I mean, I was 16 at the time. But I've always been extremely backward when it comes to transport and technology. When I first ventured onto the archaic London Underground as a boy, I was left deeply traumatised when I discovered that the trains did not have jovial, red faces on the front with names like Thomas the Tank Engine or Percy the Pink Pervert. The surreal prospect of travelling on a driverless train could only be the work of Jules Verne as far as I was concerned. So I thoroughly empathise with the Singaporean commuters who, in October 2002, suffered at the mechanical hands of the automated LRT trains, which service the HDB heartlands.

Before you could say, "Wheel, you are the weakest link, goodbye", the LRT industry almost came off the rails — for six or seven minutes. That was how long a driverless LRT train travelled along the Bukit Panjang line after a guide wheel fell off, damaging the track and causing a power trip. Stranded and seriously delayed, the shocked passengers were understandably furious.

Pragmatic officials of the SMRT system have already formulated a proposal to channel that fury. Should a train breakdown again, commuters will be able to lift individual flaps under their feet and run along the track, based on the Flintstones' model of kinetic energy. Watch how many executives will be late for work when their destiny lies in their own feet.

But to give the LRT network its due, services resumed within a couple of days. The repairs would have been quicker, but SMRT failed to agree terms with a certain Malcolm Higgins. In some circles, Higgins is revered as a technological genius. In other words, he's a sad geek who should've got out more when he was a teenager. In April 2002, he promised to rescue the British rail industry with, wait for it, a laser gun. The inventor claimed to have developed a laser beam, which could be fitted under trains to vaporise the leaves on the tracks.

Allegedly, he was sane when he made this bold claim. Though he whooped a lot and concluded by saying, "If lasers were good enough for Han Solo, then they are good enough for British Rail. Now, get your fucking hands off my gun!"

But that is the fundamental difference between Singaporean and British train services. Falling leaves can bring the entire rail network of southeast England to a standstill. In October 2000, for instance, wet leaves were blamed for a train derailment in Surrey, where the train went through a red light and just missed a commuter train. Fortunately, no one was injured, but the passengers now refuse to walk under trees during the autumnal months.

I wouldn't wish to downplay or trivialise the genuine grievances of LRT commuters of late, but if the driverless system has had just 50 problems since it began running in 1999, then it should be lauded, not lambasted.

The London Underground encounters more difficulties and breakdowns every day. According to a 2001 survey, one in 20 peak trains don't run, escalators remain broken for months and some stations have been neglected since they were built. The decaying, Victorian tube system is estimated to need 1.2 billion pounds worth of immediate investment and a further 400 million pounds annually just to keep it going. And then you have the additional problems that really are beyond the company's control.

When I was 18, I found myself virtually alone on a deserted platform at London's East Ham station. Considering it was only a couple of days before Christmas and the high street was packed with shoppers, the empty station was slightly unnerving. The station controller asked me to leave and when I asked why, he pointed to a sports bag, just two metres away and said: "Because we think that's an IRA bomb, mate."

The bag had been left under the same bloody bench that I was sitting on. It wasn't a bomb, it rarely is, but it was the fastest working laxative I've ever known.

So it is a little premature to suggest the wheels have fallen off the LRT industry. Yes, I know there was another one. But if you've survived bomb scares and the odd public battering from your mother, you're entitled to the occasional pun in your book.

Having depended on the crumbling, rat-infested London Underground to get me to school every day, I can safely say that SMRT manages the greatest public transport network I have ever known. It just needs to make its trains less impersonal. Painting smiling faces on the front and naming them Thomas or Percy has proved extremely popular. And if another wheel falls off, 'Han Solo' Higgins says he's ready with his laser gun.

NOTE: I received some criticism over this one from a Singaporean chap who thought that I was being somewhat harsh on the London Underground and that I was making an unfair comparison between the two transport models — one being modern and the other prehistoric. It's certainly true that the London Underground, built during the Victorian era, was a revolutionary, technological breakthrough in its day. And I genuinely believe that Britain is unfairly criticised for being a pioneer in many of its social policies — for instance, the London Underground, municipal housing, the welfare state and organised football. At the time, they were all sound ideas that immeasurably improved the living standards of the working classes. The said services put a roof over my head, gave me free school milk and took me to work and school every day. Indeed, the last one gave me a hobby where I could swear at 11 grown men and not get told off by my dad. Having said that, you still have to take your hat off to the Singaporean government on this one. They retained the best qualities of all of these policies and discarded the rest (the S-League being the possible exception). Being a rather late arrival into the world of nation-states, it's difficult to say whether this was by chance or design. (Singapore lacked the infrastructure to support a 'from-the-cradle-to-the-grave' system of welfare in 1965, even if it had wanted to.) Nevertheless, Britain's welfare state, like its public transport services, needs a ridiculous cash injection just to prevent its collapse in the new millennium. Why should Singaporeans care if the London Underground came first and SMRT had the benefit of hindsight garnered from another country's mistakes? Despite huge government subsidies, the London Underground loses thousands of pounds every day, while the MRT and bus services in Singapore actually turn a profit at the end of each financial year. Even if the odd wheel does fall off from time to time. But that's the reality, so be damn proud of it.

THE FREAK

ONE of the most difficult aspects about living 10,000 kilometres away from England is that my annual whirlwind visit is an exhausting trek to each of the relative outposts. I'm not complaining. I'm the selfish one who chose to live in Singapore. But it does mean, of course, the incomparable visit to my grandmother. Born just after the First World War and married by the Second, she proudly boasts that American servicemen ensured that she never needed to buy her own drinks for the full six years of conflict. A remarkable woman.

But she is a trifle off-balance. Every year, she assumes Singapore is the Asian equivalent of Hell's Island and I'm England's answer to Papillon, always seeking to escape.

"Are you still out in that place?" she begins cheerily.

"Singapore?"

"Yeah."

"Yeah."

"Shame, really. When do you think they will let you come home?"

"Nan, I love it there. I have a great job. We have lots of mates and it's a great place to live."

"Yeah, you write books and newspapers, don't you?"

"Well, sort of. But we're having a good time."

"Still, if they are pleased with all that work you are doing, they might let you come back early, right?"

"Nan, for the last time. It's a country, not a prison."

But I know she's stopped listening. That's assuming she ever paid attention in the first place. By then, she's already moved on to her mission in life — to feed her guests until they die. In this respect, she is similar to her endearing Singaporean 'auntie' counterparts. She asks the same question every year and always gets the same response.

"Would you like a sandwich, Jodie?"

"Her name's Tracy, nan."

"Sorry, Tracy. I've got ham, cornbeef, cheese. Which one would you like, Jodie?"

"She's vegetarian, nan. Remember, I told you before, right? She can't eat meat."

"Did you? On that's right. I forget everything now, silly old bastard I am... What about turkey?"

"She can't eat meat, nan."

"Oh yeah. Shame, really. When do you think you can start eating proper food again?"

"She does eat proper food, nan. She just chooses not to eat meat."

"Does she? Shame really."

We've endured the same interrogation for seven years now, so we can usually answer the questions on autopilot. But my nan's forgetfulness and harmless ignorance still left my poor girlfriend completely unprepared for the stunned reactions she gets in Singapore. Here, she is a freak. Informing friends, dinner guests and strangers generally that she is a vegetarian generates, at best, looks of puzzlement or, at worst, withering looks of contempt followed by an unpleasant grilling that wouldn't be out of place at the Internal Security Department. I've told her before that she might as well say: "I'm a cannibal. It's hereditary. I used to have seven brothers and sisters, but we ate them. So, please, eat everything up, so there's more for me later." Believe me, the horrified expressions couldn't be much worse than those she suffers now.

The negative reactions from aunties and uncles, like my grandmother, are understandable. As Singapore struggled in its formative years, putting food on the table was difficult enough. Asking for a soya burger with low-fat mayonnaise during the '60s would have been rewarded with a slap from your mother, and deservedly so. It was no different for my grandmother. During the austere post-war years, which came with ration books and coupons, housewives queued for free horsemeat because it didn't require coupons. Feeding screaming babies took precedence over saving a few well-fed hogs.

But the response to my missus' vegetarianism from the 30-somethings was more of a surprise. Singaporeans around my age often feel the need to challenge my girlfriend's moral choice. And, just like a visit to my grandmother, the same, tedious questions always come thick and fast.

"You're a vegetarian? But why?"

"Oh, it's just a personal thing. No big deal," my patient girlfriend replies.

"Are you allergic to the taste of meat?"

"No, it's not that."

"Oh, it must be religion, right. I thought so. You're part of a religion where you can't eat certain animals, right?"

"No, I'm not religious."

"Then why don't you eat meat?"

"Oh, just for the animals, you know. I don't like eating other animals."

"That's it? That's why you're a vegetarian? You want to save the animals. Ha." For some reason, this always gets a big laugh and my girlfriend always gets embarrassed. Only on one occasion have I retaliated. The 'vegetarians-are-weirdos' jokes were getting really predictable and tiresome. One of the jokers didn't eat certain meats on religious grounds and as the so-called quips developed an undercurrent of nastiness, the hypocrisy became nauseous.

"So let me get this straight," I asked. "Not eating meat on the grounds of a faith for a god we never see is tolerated. But not eating meat on the grounds of protecting actual, living creatures that we see around us every day is a subject worthy of ridicule? This hypocrisy really pisses me off."

The embarrassed silence that followed my little outburst told me I shouldn't take that subject any further and I won't here. But for many, my missus is a social freak, often treated like an invalid.

Yet she never complains. I've lost count of the times when a friend has sighed melodramatically and said: "There's great food here. Let's eat here. Oh shit, we can't, can we? We can't because I know they don't have any vegetarian dinners. Hang on, you can eat french fries, right?" Unlike a born-again Christian, she doesn't act like a born-again vegetarian, preaching to other

Singaporeans by saying: "Come follow me, people. I've found the path to enlightenment. A meatless diet will provide the key to the afterlife."

But she is a sneaky one, burrowing away quietly and laying the foundations for the future. The five-year-old kids she teaches in Singapore must be the most environmentally aware pre-school students in the world. A parent once came in and told my girlfriend that her child had lectured her for killing some cockroaches. Another student reprimanded a friend for killing a make-believe spider. A little extreme perhaps, but these little guys might just save the world that we've fucked up.

According to the academics, my girlfriend is an ovo-lacto vegetarian, which is generally the most commonly practiced dietary regime. The ovo-lacto mob won't eat any meat or fish, sticking to vegetables, eggs and dairy. That is, food products that don't involve anything with a face being killed.

Don't get me wrong, the missus doesn't want to eat anything that's a product of factory farming either. But drinking soya milk made her vomit, literally, and she lost weight at an alarming rate. Finding free-range products is possible here, but it's about as likely as telling the average Singaporean that you're a vegetarian and not getting the piss taken out of you.

That's why I admire her. It's so difficult to be a vegetarian here, especially if you're not a big fan of vegetables in the first place, which she isn't. I couldn't do it. In the West and Australia, a vegetarian culture has mushroomed over the last 10 years or so. In supermarkets, whole aisles are devoted to mock meats and various meals for vegetarians. Even vegans, who avoid all dairy products and won't wear anything that is derived from an animal, are well catered for in the West.

Indeed, it has become hip for younger Westerners to denounce meat-eating. According to a *TIME* survey in July 2002, some 10 million Americans consider themselves to be practising vegetarians and another 20 million have flirted with a meat-free diet. And this is a country where babies are born in hotdog buns and thrown onto the barbeque at a very young age. If it ain't got a pulse, they ain't gonna eat it. Indeed, the country certainly has the best damn steak that I've ever tasted. Yet 25 per cent of adolescents polled by Teenage Research Unlimited in America said vegetarianism was "sensible" and "cool", according to *TIME* magazine.

There are also health reasons. Aside from the usual additives, there is that fun stuff in meat like the E. Coli bacteria and Britain's contribution to fine dining — Mad Cow Disease. Do you remember reading about that? Britain's mooing population started staggering around with their underpants on their head and barking at their farmers, who were feeding them the remains of just about every other animal species on the planet. The poor cows were deranged. I remember one being interviewed on TV about the disease and he replied: "Mad cows? Never heard of it, mate. I'm an octopus. Do you want to see my tentacles?"

To be fair, my grandmother continued to eat meat during the Mad Cows furore and there was no discernible difference in her behaviour. But then, this is a woman who would perform her Hawaiian dance without invitation and flash her knickers to anyone who was foolish enough to watch. Had she contracted the virus, it might have been nigh on impossible to spot the symptoms. Despite piles of dead cows all over the English countryside, it still took some time for the missus' family to come to terms with her vegetarianism. But eventually they did, albeit reluctantly.

But in Singapore she remains a social outcast. The nation has an entrenched food culture that it is fiercely proud and protective of, and rightly so. The plethora of choice at any decent hawker centre or food court puts Singapore in the food Premiership. In England, you can have fish with chips, meat with chips and chips with chips at most food courts. And when the hungry pay a visit to their local Indian or Chinese takeaway in England — they order chips. I cannot think of any English environment, where there can be at least 15 to 20 completely different dishes all under one roof. I have seen it in the United States, but not, I'm afraid, in the southeast of England.

There is a tendency, however, to become too protective of one's culture. Some Singaporeans can be very elitist when it comes to their dishes. Fish is my Singaporean failing. I simply don't like it. I never have and I never will. End of story. But it isn't. It's never allowed to be in Singapore. Lengthy explanations are required to pacify your host and dinner guests; occasionally, it gets offensive. I have been told so many times: "You know, it's actually quite rude not to eat a dish that's been prepared for you." I should reply: "You know, in England, it's actually quite rude to humiliate someone in front of friends and strangers at a dinner table. You know, in England, it's actually customary for me to smack you in your mouth about now." But, of course, I refrain. I bite my tongue instead. That way, it becomes numb and I can no longer taste the fish.

So I have a confession to make. For seven years now, I've been living a lie. It's time for me to come clean, publicly, in this book. I'm not really allergic to fish. It doesn't liquify my bodily waste and leave me sitting on the toilet for four hours. Nor does it make my eyes weep a yellow pus. Nor does it render me impotent. I've used all of these stories and more to pacify my dinner company, when they enquire about my non-fish eating. It's a last-ditch attempt to thwart the oncoming sales pitch. But it rarely works.

You see, if I don't like the fish, my eating companions often try to 'sell' it to me. When informed that I don't like fish, they look as if I've just stepped off a spaceship and reply: "But it's been cooked steamboat style, you know. It's really good."

"I believe you, but I just don't really like fish. I never have."

"I know. But this tastes different. It's cooked in a steamboat."

"I understand. But it wouldn't matter if it was cooked in a canoe."

"But it's been steamed. It's been fried. It's been grilled. It's been boiled. It's been baked, barbequed and roasted. It's been firebombed and it's one of Singapore's most famous dishes, you know."

"I'm really sorry." And then comes my favourite.

"This fish is very expensive, you know."

"Look, it doesn't matter if the fish has the brains of Free Willy, the figure of the Little Mermaid, has been boiled in liquid gold for 15 years and you had to sell your HDB flat to buy two kilograms, I really don't like fish."

That's when the comments usually come in about offending the cook, the custom, or the festival and how this *ang moh* doesn't understand local culture. I do. I really do. I just don't eat fish. That's about as complicated as it gets. But that food protectorate is ever present. I rarely eat Western food, unless the girls at the office bring some back, because it's too expensive. Yet the second a french fry touches my lips, someone from the Food Force seems to be on hand to say, "Why don't you try fish ball noodles, *roti john*, *nasi padang*, chicken rice, *rojak* or *satay*? There's so much more to eat than just burgers." You don't say.

Yet I've got Chinese friends who won't go near an Indian or a Muslim stall. I had a late night supper of chicken curry at an Indian stall, while a Chinese friend tactlessly informed me that he'd never order from a stall like that. I know Indians who have never eaten fish ball noodles in their life. And I once asked a Malay friend to pick up some *char siew fun* from the coffee shop and he didn't know what barbecued pork rice was, even after I'd explained it to him. Yet, because my girlfriend is a vegetarian and I don't take fish, we're the ones who get criticised for not assimilating into another man's culture? The hypocrisy is astounding. But we can't even go there, can we? Religious and racial harmony and all that. Let's not rock the steamboat. Point the finger at the *ang moh* instead. There will be less repercussions and, ultimately, it's safer.

That's why my girlfriend's vegetarianism is a testament to her patience. Having endured disparaging comments for over four years, she's coped remarkably well. I would join her, but I know I would end up punching someone. Besides, as I'm always cruelly reminding the missus, mutton *korma*, *nasi briyani* and beef *kway teow* all taste so bloody good, don't they?

But the mood is changing. Most Singaporean teenagers wouldn't consider vegetarians as freaks. The younger generations are increasingly spurning sharks fin soup, refusing to serve it at their wedding dinners. Singapore will evolve quite nicely in the hands of these brave, politically aware heroes of mine.

They've watched the documentaries. They've witnessed what a despicable, bloody process removing the shark's fin is. It's hardly clinical. The sharks are often baited with fish and smashed over the head by the fishermen to keep them from struggling. The fins are hacked off in a pretty haphazard fashion and the shark is thrown back into the sea. Like mammals who have lost a limb, the shark will soldier on for a day or two in excruciating pain before succumbing to its fatal injuries.

Without its fin, the imbalanced shark struggles to swim properly and he either drowns or bleeds to death. It is an agonisingly slow and painful death. The old *Jaws* argument that sharks fin soup ensures that mankind has one less man-eating predator to worry about is utter nonsense. Shark attacks usually account for around 50 human deaths a year. They are usually accidental, with the shark often mistaking a surfboard for an injured seal. To avenge this statistic, man is responsible for around 100 million shark deaths a year, according to Wild Aid. That sounds fair.

Yet, for these wonderful Singaporeans, it's not just about saving the sharks. These guys face tremendous parental and peer pressure to maintain 'face' and follow Chinese tradition. Sharks fin soup, once served up by the Chinese aristocracy, represents affluence and wealth. In extreme cases of parental dogma, they risk alienation. To the older generations, not serving the traditional 10-course meal with all the usual dishes would be about as popular as not serving alcohol at a British wedding. But the couples are valiantly sticking to their guns and sharks fin soup is no longer the status symbol it perhaps once was. Just as it's 'cool' among teenagers in America not to eat meat, it's becoming 'cool' in Singapore not to serve Jaws' broth at wedding dinners. I'm probably biased because you already know my stance on fish. But sharks fin soup tastes like cat's piss to me so I'm all for keeping it off the menu.

Moreover, public awareness, again among younger Singaporeans, concerning issues such as the environment, animal rights and the crumbling ecosystems is spreading rapidly. I know the government would like to take credit for this with their countless campaigns and community slogans, but the answer is far simpler — cable television. When I was a child, Ronald McDonald was an icon on television. Today, Singaporean children watch crocodile hunter Steve Irwin remind them that the ugliest lizard they've even seen, which is usually green, has three horns, five eyes and a protruding sphincter, is still a "beauty" that must be respected and protected.

It was cable television that converted the missus. At times, I don't know whether to celebrate or curse the day the Animal Planet Channel arrived in our living room. Normally, the soppy woman cries when Forrest Gump loses his mother or when ET leaves Earth, which actually makes the alien a 'quitter' in the eyes of the Singaporean government. But she cried me a river when *Animal Hospital* failed to save an iguana called Colin. And she is not alone. In HDB flats across Singapore, children are learning about the ecosystems of the South American rainforests on the Discovery Channel, the emotional intelligence of elephants on the National Geographic Channel and the lack of emotional intelligence of Steve Irwin on Animal Planet.

Ironically, the Singaporean government resisted satellite television for years, fearing uncensored filth, pornography and sleazy behaviour would be beamed into our homes. But no one wants to watch the daily session of Britain's House of Lords anyway. Instead, the government can hope that it might just end up with a generation of global citizens aware of issues beyond the economic sphere, who respect the moral choices of others. Not because the government tells them to, in the interests of religious and racial harmony, but simply because their understanding tells them it's the right thing to do.

I'm not saying that they should, or will, become vegetarians. That would be grossly hypocritical because, at the moment, I'm not one. But the new kids on Singapore's block will be more informed and less inclined to say: "You don't eat meat or fish? Never mind *lah*, you can eat this. It's chilli crab."

THE TOURIST

THE Bangkok weather was surprisingly cool; the riverboat was cruising along the Chao Phraya River and my view was obscured by an arse that could have covered Mount Everest.

Prior to booking the Bangkok boat trip a couple of years back, I hadn't realised that the Pentax pair were also coming. You've met them, right? They're those red-faced *ang moh* tourists, usually American, with a penchant for floral shirts and knee-high white socks with sandals. They speak only one language — touristese — and they speak it loudly.

On that Bangkok trip, they bellowed comments like: "Gee, Mary Jane, I got me a real Thai pauper here. He ain't wearing nothing but a pair of ripped shorts and a toothless grin. He's doing his laundry in the river. You see him, Mary Jane? Come on, honey, get your glasses on and get yourself some culture here. You see him? Right there, in front of his wooden stick house. Be quick now, Mary Jane, I got me the long lens on my Pentax ready, so you just wave and get that peasant to wave right back."

The Thai economy depends on the Pentax pair and their tourist brothers and sisters worldwide to bring in foreign currencies, by selling the more intimate aspects of its culture. And now, Singapore wants to do the same.

In March 2003, the Singapore Tourism Board announced that it was contemplating taking over two vacant HDB blocks in Tiong Bahru Road so it could transform them into budget hotels. The idea is that tourists will scratch beneath Singapore's superficial veneer to gain a greater understanding of real, heartland life. The scheme is aimed primarily at an increasingly affluent and jet-setting middle class in China, because they're big spenders here. They are only in Singapore for a couple of days, but, apparently, they whip out the credit card more frequently than most other tourists, including the Americans and the British.

Well, the average Chinese teenager must be beside himself with excitement after hearing of the Singapore Tourism Board's plans here. "So let me get this straight, mum," he will say, in Mandarin. "You want us to get on a plane, fly to Singapore... to look at people... living in tower blocks. No wait, that's not quite correct, is it? You want us to look at predominately Chinese people living in tower blocks. Now that's something I've never done before. Do you think I could rebook that appointment to have my irritable bowel removed?"

Don't get me wrong. I'm all for tourists moving away from the colonial track and the spectre of Stamford Raffles. It takes a week just to visit every statue, street, monument, school and so forth with the man's bloody name on it. I don't know about you, but I have better things to do with my time than listen to Singaporean tour guides say: "And on my left is a statue of a fat British imperialist with silly sideburns. And on my right is a street named after a fat British imperialist with silly sideburns.

Indeed, in the days of the British Empire, Charles Dickens and public floggings, it was considered necessary for imperialists to be fat and have silly sideburns. They were prerequisites for the job. Public servants were required to resemble the Empire's ruler — Queen Victoria."

And while we're on the subject of Singaporean sightseeing, the city-state certainly has more to offer than the Merlion, which is the nation's tourism symbol. Once the initial, disturbing image of a cross-dressing lion wears off, there is little to be excited about other than its basic plumbing.

"Look at the Merlion spewing water. Isn't it fabulous, kids?" Desperate tourists ask their distinctly unimpressed children as they glide along the Singapore River.

"Yeah, mum. But our shower does that every day and we don't all stand under that to take pictures, do we? If we did, mum, you'd be arrested. And another thing, mum, does this mean that Singapore was created when a randy Lion shagged a hormonal mermaid on the banks of the Singapore River?"

Undoubtedly, providing the coach parties with more sightseeing options is certainly an admirable plan. But are the HDB heartlands of housing blocks the place to go? I can imagine the poor guide travelling past my block in Toa Payoh.

"And on my left, ladies and gentlemen, we have the large troughs for leaflets and flyers. There has been a misconception, judging by the pungent smell, among those who believe them to be urinals. They are, in fact, a place to throw junk mail for lazy bastards who cannot walk two metres to the nearest dustbin."

But, to be honest, the notion of affluent tourists snapping away at HDB dwellers is both intrusive and patronising and I speak from experience on this one.

Last year, some bright spark decided that my old hometown — that east London borough called Dagenham — was a suitable tourist destination. Having lived there for 20 years, I have no idea what the attraction is, but guided tours now snake around the streets. Coaches actually travel past the countless, two-storey terraced houses, which once formed the world's largest municipal housing estate. There were rumours that some coach drivers actually got lost because every house looks the bloody same. The biggest mistake, though, was playing Groundhog Day on the coach's video. Three Japanese tourists had a nervous breakdown that day.

Aside from town planners and die-hard fans of Dudley Moore and Terry Venables (who were both born in Dagenham), it's difficult to know what attracts sightseers to the place. You must understand that when the eyesore was designed in the 1920s, the London County Council's architect obviously built the original model from Lego. Unfortunately, he only had red bricks left. Singaporeans might deride the monotony of HDB estates, but at least your blocks differ in shape and size.

Apparently, Dagenham tour guides say things like: "On your left is Parsloes Park, a popular place for drunken teenagers to have sex and catch frostbite on their arses. Contraception is optional, ladies and gentlemen, and you might be interested to know that the London Borough of Barking and Dagenham has one of the highest rates of teenage pregnancy in Britain, which, in turn, has one of the highest teenage pregnancy rates in Europe. So you're actually witnessing a social phenomenon here, you lucky devils."

"And on your right is the Robin Hood Pub, a popular place for drug dealers, drunken brawls and police raids. Though, in fairness, the pub does serve a bloody good pint of lager and a decent sausage sandwich."

I'm all for a greater understanding of another man's culture, but when you intrude upon the working man's abode, whether it be in Bangkok, Tiong Bahru Road or Dagenham, it's not tourism; it's just bloody *kaypoh*. We already have burglar alarms and grills on our windows to prevent unwelcome intruders from stopping by in the dead of night. Now, if you take the Singapore Tourism Board's grand scheme to its logical conclusion, we've got to contend with chattering tourists in floral shirts shuffling along our corridors and poking their sunburnt noses through our windows.

Would you want patronising coach parties turning up at your HDB block? Should the Pentax pair pay a visit to my home asking to take a cultural photograph of "the working-class *ang moh* hanging out the washing", I will allow them to take just one, of a certain part of my anatomy, which I will then invite them to kiss. And you just know where that bamboo pole is going to end up...

THE CASINO

THE disturbed auntie was clearly unwell. Attempting to look through a crack in the door no more than 5 mm wide, the elderly Singaporean shouted: "*Oi*, what time you open, *ah*? Can come in or not?"

Unsurprisingly, the crack in the door failed to reply. The auntie's daughter, obviously embarrassed by a mother who likes bending over to talk to inanimate objects in public places, made an attempt to shoo the elderly woman away. It failed. So she made a last-ditch appeal to the auntie's dwindling common sense.

"Mama," she started. "The casino will not open until we reach international waters."

"International Waters," came the reply. "Where's that, ah?"

I had only just been welcomed aboard a luxurious, five-star cruise ship when I stumbled upon this family cabaret.

A fortnight earlier, my company said that it wouldn't mind paying for its staff to enjoy an all-inclusive weekend cruise along the coast of Malaysia. What could I say? If *TODAY* newspaper wanted to celebrate its second birthday by feeding me six times a day in opulent luxury, then I would just have to grin and bear it.

But I love cruise ships and all their inimitable quirks. Where else in the world can you be fined for throwing "foreign objects" down the toilet? Sitting on the 'throne', I read a warning that stipulated that "foreign objects" could cause a blockage and my room would be charged $200 to pay for the plumber.

Terrified, I almost ran out into the corridor to check with a chambermaid. But I reasoned that the sight of a semi-naked Caucasian running at you with his trousers around his ankles, waving his tackle about while holding a toilet roll and screaming: "Was this made in Singapore? Is it a Singaporean toilet roll?" might be a tad disconcerting.

The ship's telephone operator was also in a league of her own. Eager to speak to a couple of mates, I called and said: "Can I have the room number of Kenneth Goh please?"

"I'm sorry, he's not on our guest list," the breezy operator replied quickly. "Do you know his Chinese name?"

I didn't, so I tried another mate.

"No, I can't find a Mr. Leonard Thomas on the list either," said the cheery operator. "Do you happen to know his Chinese name?"

Cruise tickets may not always be inexpensive, but comments like that are priceless. Playing in the ship's casino, however, does come at a price. Forget the swimming pools and the lounge singers; for many passengers, the wonderful vessel is just a floating Singaporean casino. It's tragic, but that's the reality, and that's not good for the industry's family-oriented image. So according to the ship's flyer, there really wasn't a casino covering half of one of its decks. There was an entertainment area that provided "games of chance" instead. So I turned up ready to play a quiet game of Monopoly.

What are "games of chance" anyway? It's rather like saying Geylang's brothels provide "activities of pleasure". The only difference being you are likely to spend a hell of lot more money on the former, than you would on the latter — unless you have the sexual voracity of a well-hung stallion, of course. But these "games of chance" do not exactly appeal to the most positive traits of the average Singaporean gambler.

"I know I shouldn't say this, but the Singaporeans are very *kiasu* when it comes to gambling," said the ship's food and beverage director, a rather harried Malaysian chap.

"We aim to open our restaurants half an hour before the designated times to reduce queueing. Then we avoid pushing and shouting matches. Many want to get into the casino as soon as possible, you see."

"Couldn't you install a turnstile that connected the casino to the restaurant?" I offered, unhelpfully.

"No," he replied. "They'd break it getting in."

And that's when I discovered it's all a question of timing. The discerning punter knows that the casino cannot operate until the ship reaches international waters, so he eats quickly before the doors are opened.

Many passengers are unconcerned, or even unaware, of the ship's course or eventual destination. Under the cloak of darkness, the captain should spend the twilight hours circling Sentosa endlessly. Gamblers wouldn't notice the difference. Passengers who notice the Merlion in their porthole for the seventeenth time will just put it down to either seasickness or alcohol. I'm not kidding. When I was checking out at 11.15am, a passenger asked what time the ship would arrive back in Singapore.

"At 11am, madam," came the stunned reply. "We docked 15 minutes ago."

I acknowledged the woman's acute observational powers by poking her in the eye with my cardkey as she left.

When I visited the casino at 1am and again at 9am, it was never less than packed. And on both occasions, I saw the mad, gambling auntie telling everyone "what a great holiday resort this International Waters" was. That's the reality. So why on earth is the government stalling on the proposal to legitimise casinos in Singapore?

In the latter part of 2002, the Tourism Working Group, a government-appointed task force said it was time for one or two "games of chance" to be set up on Sentosa.

Calls to build a casino came about during the last recession in 1985-6. It's a guaranteed money-spinner. Local betting revenues generated $500 million during the soccer World Cup.

I don't gamble, but I don't begrudge people who do. So I say to the chaps in government: Build a casino on an exclusive Sentosa resort, tax it and if my insane auntie friend wants to fritter away her life savings on the roulette wheel, then so be it. And if it offends your personal or religious beliefs, then don't go. The cruise proved that Singaporeans will never stop gambling, so the government might as well cash in on it. But most importantly of all, I discovered that foreign objects should never come into contact with one's bottom.

NOTE: I've been to casinos in Las Vegas, Perth, Malaysia's Genting Highlands and on a cruise liner and I've always met Singaporeans. And my mother has just told me that she visited a casino near her home in Ramsgate, Kent, which is a seaside resort tucked away in the south corner of England and she ended up chatting with some Singaporeans there! When it comes to the English Premiership, the millions of dollars that are generated by illegal football betting in this tiny island is nothing short of obscene. And that will never change. I know there are religious sensitivities to consider. But I can't believe that the Singaporean government, which has to be the most fiscally minded on the planet, is still content to allow these vast revenues to be lost on someone else's blackjack tables.

THE WAR

I HATE Saddam Hussein. Given the opportunity, I would gladly pull out his moustache hairs with a pair of rusty pliers. I have nothing against men (or women) with moustaches, you understand, just men with moustaches who also happen to be murderous tyrants. Using the examples of Josef Stalin, Adolf Hitler and Omar Sharif, my mother sat me down when I was five years old and said: "Neil, never trust a man with a moustache."

With the benefit of hindsight, I suspect her jaundiced view was due to the fact that my parents had just divorced and my father had fashioned a trendy hairstyle on his upper lip during the marriage. He went for Tom Selleck in *Magnum*, but bore a closer resemblance to George Harrison in *Sgt. Pepper*.

I know Hitler was responsible for the Holocaust and Stalin engineered the Great Terror, but my father often came home pissed on a Friday night, so you can see where my mother was coming from. But "Mad-ass" Hussein is a different kettle of moustaches altogether. On Friday, March 21st, 2003, that evil bastard made me walk down 28 flights of stairs.

Since the world was plunged into yet another war, security

measures have become even more stringent in Singapore. Yes, I know, the conflict really only involves Iraq, the United States, Britain and a few stragglers, but Americans have a habit of singing songs like "We Are The World". Say no more.

But with the disobedient Hussein refusing to die, as instructed by the Texan in the White House, Singapore has been forced to tighten its belt and keep its citizens on its toes. So on that fateful Friday, at 2pm, there was a fire drill in the office. Over the PA system, a robotic, but strangely sexy, female voice said: "This is a fire drill. Imagine the place is being ravaged by flames and you are choking on the smoke and everyone around you is screaming: 'Get out of the fucking way, you dopey prick, there's a fire'. Well, ignore all that and make your way slowly to the staircases."

I finished my sandwich and read the paper. There was hardly a mad stampede for the door. I expected John Cleese's hotel manager, Basil Fawlty, to storm in and shout: "I don't know why we bother, we should let you all burn."

I don't wish to sound flippant, but it's difficult to take fire drills seriously. We all know that in the event of a real fire, we'd all be running around like headless chickens and thinking: "Now, if I boot that dithering auntie out of the way, push over that meandering woman who's carrying four children and knock out that uncle with the fire extinguisher, I should be the first one down the stairs."

And, may I ask, have you ever attempted a brisk walk down 28 flights of non-air-conditioned stairs at 2pm in the humid afternoon? If the government posted Newater officials at the exit at the bottom of the stairs, the water dispute with Malaysia would be settled immediately. They could just wring us out.

Indeed, there should have been water stations on the way down, like those in the Singapore Marathon. Every 10 floors, volunteers should hand out isotonic drinks and shout words of encouragement, such as: "Come on, you sweaty, red-faced *ang moh* prick. Stop ogling equally sweaty secretaries and get a bloody move on."

I wouldn't mind, but my fellow evacuees and I were not even awarded certificates or rosettes when we made it out into the dazzling sunshine. At the very least, the soundtrack to *Chariots of Fire* could have been played over the PA system. And security guards could have held up a silk ribbon so we could "breast the tape" as we crossed the finish line.

Why is the Singapore government wasting its time with the National Healthy Lifestyle Campaign and investing in sports stadiums, running tracks and subsidised gymnasiums for national servicemen? Organise two fire drills a week and Singapore will become the fittest country on the planet. It is certainly the most attractive, at least during the time of war. Since the Iraqi conflict began, Singaporeans have been flocking to the hairdressers, according to an informed source of mine. The day after the fire drill, I was taken off the glucose drip and released from hospital, so I thought I'd treat myself to a haircut. I waited two hours. Two bloody hours. When I asked Alvin, my hairdresser, why he was so busy, he replied: "Don't know man, it's been like that since the war started."

And it wasn't even self-conscious men lining up to have their moustaches shaved off. The room was full of women, predominately aunties, all sitting there having trims, washes and perms. Some were even sitting under those huge helmet-like radio headsets, listening, I presume, to the latest news on

Iraq. But how did this come to pass?

Did concerned aunties watch the outbreak of hostilities on TV, call their friends and say: "*Ah Soh*, it's started. It looks like Baghdad won't fall for another month. We better go get our hair coloured. Yep, it's that serious."

Perhaps they meet friends and say: "Love your tight perm. You had that done after allied forces entered Basra, didn't you? Yeah, me too. No choice, right?"

Discussing haircuts and fire drills might appear insensitive during a time of war, but life must go on. I know, because Nicole Kidman told me so on TV, during the recent Oscar ceremony.

Besides, I'd rather talk about moustaches than money, which seems to be the most popular topic of discussion in Singapore since the allied forces started bombing Baghdad. I swear if one more dull Singaporean tells me that people dying in Iraq is going to weaken the strength of the dollar in the pocket, I will gag them with a two-dollar bill.

Singaporeans, who have been polled on the streets by the various media for their views during the war, have come out with some real crackers, such as: "We must be prudent with our spending", "Our recession is going to get worse", "This war is bound to affect our pockets" and "I'm a boring bastard obsessed with economics".

While the world is hitting the streets to protest against an unjust war, what are these people doing? To be fair, six Singaporeans attempted to stage a peace protest outside the American Embassy on the eve of the war, but were stopped by plain-clothes policemen. Apparently, two of the protesters were checked by police before they had even taken their peace placards out of their bags. These are wonderfully courageous

Singaporeans. It's impossible to feel anything other than admiration for such global citizens.

But what about these fiscal fuckers fretting over their bank accounts? What did they do during the Iraqi conflict — sit at home and count their money on a calculator? Perhaps I'm missing the point because when I was at school, I only used calculators to write the word "boobs" on the screen. That always impressed the girls.

I'm not seeking to tempt fate here, but should an invading army ever make its way through Malaysia and across the Causeway, I often wonder how the money-minded will react. Perhaps then, those mass protests for peace that were held all over the planet, except in Singapore, of course, won't appear so futile. Perhaps then, the greedy gang will accept that, in most cases, one's savings book is not a bullet-proof vest.

Aside from moustaches, my mother always told me it was uncouth to discuss money matters publicly. But to selfishly lament the weakness of your country's dollar because citizens elsewhere have the impudence to die is so staggeringly inhumane, it is beyond comprehension.

After the terrorist attack on the twin towers in New York in 2001, I remember a Singaporean friend expressing his concern. He worked for an American corporation and knew that September 11th would damage the American economy. We were discussing the tragedy when he said: "Never mind the attack; I didn't know the people who died. All I know is, this is going to really fuck up the American dollar. Our company is really going to struggle because of this fucking thing."

You can't talk to these wankers. You can't rationalise with them. How do they sleep at night? I just cannot understand, let alone tolerate their logic.

To keep your sanity, I would advise you to steer well clear of these people. Personally, at a time of war, I'd rather get my hair coloured at Alvin's hairdressers with the mad aunties. Their actions make more sense to me.

THE AMERICANS

I'M NOT sure whether it was the blustery winds, the lack of warm clothes or a combination of both because I wasn't my usual, tolerant self. For some reason, I wanted to rip out the American lady's vocal cords and strangle her with them. A little harsh, perhaps, but she never stopped bloody talking.

I was in the United States to interview an actor because his upcoming movie was about to be released in Singapore. I'd never been to New York before, but to me it was the movie capital of the world. Like many Singaporeans, I'd seen its famous landmarks in so many films and TV programmes, I felt like I'd lived there.

Naturally, I wanted to see as many of its famous sites as I could during my whirlwind 48-hour trip. As soon as it was daylight on a brisk November morning, I headed for the Statue of Liberty. The old lady had terrorised me as a child when I saw her sticking out of the sand in the post-apocalyptic world of the Planet of the Apes. I still expected to find a distraught Charlton Heston banging the ground in bitter frustration, wearing nothing but a loincloth. Instead, I found a daft old bat from Kansas who rattled my eardrums.

From the moment we left Manhattan, I suffered her mindless chatter across the choppy Hudson River all the way to Liberty Island. Initially, she seemed almost normal.

"Gee, doesn't the Statue of Liberty look fantastic?" she asked.

"Yes, she looks good," I muttered.

"Gee, you're not from round here are ya?"

When I concurred that I came from England, she spewed the kind of verbal diarrhoea usually reserved for parliamentarians.

"Gee, England?" she began. "I love your train stations. They're just great. Gee, I thought Harry Potter was fictitious. I never knew that all the stations really were like that. They're the same. Where is Hogwarts Station? Is there a real one?"

"Oh yes, of course," I replied. "It's in Kent."

"Gee, really? I guessed as much. Gee, that's real cool."

"Excuse me, if you say 'gee' one more time, would you be awfully offended if I smacked you with my souvenir Statue of Liberty figurine?"

I didn't really say the last part. The figurine was a gift for someone and it was quite expensive. But Americans do say the daftest things. They certainly help to put Singlish into perspective.

Fearful of the social stigma attached to a 'street' dialect, Singaporeans are often worried about being pigeonholed with the lower classes if their sentences are littered with the odd *lah, aiyoh* and *referee kayu*.

Well, stop fretting over it because the Americans, particularly New Yorkers, really don't care what they say or how they say it. They, too, have their own dialect and, unlike some Singaporeans, they are most proud of it. It's called shouting. If human beings came with built-in remote controls, then God would hit the mute button on New Yorkers. They love to say what they think — though not always in that order.

Having lived in both England and Singapore, two conservative societies by comparison, it is both intimidating and invigorating. New Yorkers want to share their opinions with the world. Stunned to learn the Statue of Liberty was closed, I asked a gum-chewing park ranger why. Without hesitation, he replied: "Because of those bastard terrorists."

Well, quite. Fortunately, his colleague, a rather buxom woman, who never stopped eating, had a readymade solution. "Find a field," she said. "And stick George Bush and Saddam Hussein in it. Then let them punch each other out. They obviously have issues, right? So let them beat the crap out of each other and leave us out of it. If that don't work, stick 'em on Jerry Springer."

Being a contentious issue, I kept quiet. Fortunately, her geopolitical views had been shared with just 500 other tourists of all nationalities. We were waiting in line for a full body search, which involved being patted down by a young man, who seemed to pat far more zealously around the groin area.

Understandably, since September 11 the heavy hand of security can be felt everywhere. It's a constant reminder of the tragedy. Eager to pay my respects, I tried to locate Ground Zero, but it was hidden among Manhattan's labyrinth of streets and avenues. When I thought I'd spotted it, I asked a Wall Street trader if I was right.

He said: "What you mean is that big hole in the middle of the street with cranes and construction guys everywhere? I'm thinking — yes, you've found it."

He wasn't being flippant or insensitive. Tourists posing for holiday snaps in front of the devastated site — that's insensitive. Street vendors selling framed photographs and t-shirts of the disaster right beside Ground Zero — that's insensitive. This guy, like most New Yorkers, just wants to return to some semblance of normalcy.

There is a discernable citywide effort to become bolder and brasher than ever before. This is positively terrifying: New Yorkers were bold and brash in the first place. If you don't believe me, just ask one of them for directions. I did — and I'm suing the bastard for causing deafness in one ear.

"Waddaya wanna go to the Chrysler Building for?" He bellowed. "The Empire State Building's got a viewing platform. No? Okay, you gotta make a left on 59th, then a right on 38th, a zigzag on 5th, followed by a hot shoe shuffle on 42nd. Then cross to 9th and make over to 63rd."

"Now, take away the number you first started with and waddaya got?"

It was like doing one of those silly mental arithmetic games when I was in school. And it's exhausting work — enough to make you say 'gee', in fact. But that's not advisable.

There are enough Singaporeans with phoney American accents as it is. In the United States, it's their mother tongue and they still say the daftest things. So don't tell the government, but you're better off with Singlish, don't you think? Anyway, I'd better stop there. I'm meeting my family at Hogwarts Station.

NOTE: An irate American reader said I had no right to pigeonhole New Yorkers, or worse yet, over 250 million Americans as being 'daft' after spending just one weekend in Manhattan. He's absolutely right, of course. Powerful, intelligent Americans have contributed so much to the world — hot-dogs, hula-hoops, American football, the list is just endless. Take the most powerful man in America, the president. He's not a daft man, is he? He never says funny or peculiar things. I mean, as the leader of the people, he can't. Though I still think there is a 'u' missing in that last word. Incidentally, I had a Singaporean friend who spent a year studying in the United States and returned sounding like Jennifer Aniston. She hasn't spoken to me since this article came out. That's strange. Perhaps she's been busy.

THE SPY

I WAS walking past New York's Bloomingdales department store when it hit me. There is one man who can resurrect Singapore's economy.

The Ministry of Trade and Industry has been churning out depressing figures of late regarding the Gross Dyslexic Peacock and all those other exciting economic statistics. So allow me to add a positive figure of my own — 007. Don't worry. The suave super-spy will stir up the Singaporean economy and shake it to its very foundations no less.

To celebrate the 40th anniversary of Ian Fleming's creation on the silver screen, Bloomingdales had a mini-Bond exhibition on display in its store windows during the 2002 Christmas period. After 20 official movies, it's no less than the British naval commander deserves.

But then it occurred to me. When was the last time you saw the dapper gentleman in Singapore? You haven't. In over 40 hours of screen time, his polished brogues have never set foot on the Changi Airport runway.

The Republic has been mentioned though, twice in fact. In Sean Connery's *You Only Live Twice* and Pierce Brosnan's *Tomorrow Never Dies*, spy chief M refers to "our satellite in Singapore".

Now, where is this top-secret satellite and who the hell is operating it on behalf of Britain's Secret Service? It's probably an illegal bookie living in Toa Payoh, trying to receive the English Premiership on ESPN without paying for it. But seriously, I'm going to impart classified information and reveal the satellite's location. It's at the summit of Bukit Timah Hill. Have you noticed that fenced off "military" area at the top? There are those graphic signs, depicting a matchstick man being shot for trespassing.

Should you pass that deterrent, there is another sign, showing a trespassing matchstick man having his testicles removed with an MRT farecard. (You might as well do something with them now that the ez-link card has mercilessly replaced them.)

That's where MI6 is hiding its communicative hardware for Southeast Asia! But who's operating the satellite — the monkeys? Surely they can't be running the intelligence agencies of both London and Singapore? Luckily, this isn't the case. Sources at the Internal Security Department intercepted a recent transmission sent out from Bukit Timah.

The male voice said: "M? It's Beng in Singapore. Getting interference *lah*, cannot *lah*. Trying to watch Man Yoo. Big game *lah*, half ball some more. Get that *'ham-sum' ang moh* called Bond James Bond can? Let him fix problem, so can watch match in peace."

That's right. Get Bond out here. Let's have the franchise's producers, the Broccoli family, bring their US$100 million budget to Singapore and allow the Republic to be the exotic Asian location for the 21st instalment.

Japan (*You Only Live Twice*), Hong Kong, Thailand (*The Man with the Golden Gun*), Vietnam (*Tomorrow Never Dies*) and now Korea (*Die Another Day*) have all been featured in the Bond series. Thailand actually renamed the island used in Roger Moore's *The Man with the Golden Gun*, calling it the James Bond Island. Its near Phuket and tourists flock to it every week.

And what does Singapore have after 20 high-tech Bond movies? A satellite. But all that's going to change. In the next movie, the world's favourite spy will be met, in the customary fashion, by the local operative at Changi Airport. Pierce Brosnan will step into the Singaporean sunshine and mutter the immortal words: "My name's Bond. James Bond. Licensed to kill."

"My name's Beng. *Ah Beng*," his opposite number will reply. "Licensed to squat on MRT trains."

They can compare drinks — Bond has his martini "shaken, not stirred", Beng has his Tiger Beer "bottled, no cup". And consider their wardrobes. Bond's handmade suits are bought from a tailor in upmarket Chelsea. Beng gets his matching white singlet and trousers from a night market in Choa Chu Kang.

Moreover, setting the movie in an unfamiliar Asian location will inject fresh impetus into an ageing franchise. We've all seen the ski chases, the car crashes and the jump from Paris' Eiffel Tower in *A View To A Kill*. We can all do that.

Get Bond to jump off an HDB block and see if he can open his parachute in time. Now that's a stunt sequence. Should he fail, at least Singapore can boast that it was the country that finally killed 007. And *Ah Beng* can pick his 4-D lottery numbers based upon the floor his dead colleague jumped from.

Then there's the diabolical megalomaniac. Thirsting for totalitarian control, the Bond villain must be contemptuous of his underlings and dismissive of his opponents.

Oh dear. Do you think Singapore could fit all its "villains" into one movie? But I'm opting for the durian seller. *In Live and Let Die*, Tee Hee had his hook, while Oddjob had his bowler hat in *Goldfinger*. In the Singapore movie, the durian seller will have his *parang*.

The dastardly cad would allow Bond, who is so enamoured with the double entendre, to deliver throwaway lines like: "Well, Durian. I like your aftershave. And is that a *parang* in your trousers or are you just pleased to see me?"

And if the director needs beautiful, but one-dimensional, women to fawn over Bond, then he should head for Orchard Towers. Two hours and a large wallet should do the trick.

Whatever way you look at it, all the essential ingredients for a formulaic 007 movie are here in plentiful abundance. It's time for the Singapore Tourism Industry to bring Bond to Bras Basah. And "Bra Bizarre", incidentally, makes a great name for a Bond girl.

Should you get a chance to watch the latest Bond offering again, watch the end titles closely because I understand the next movie will have a poignant plot twist. The final credits will read: "The end of *Die Another Day*. But James Bond will return in *Ah Beng Die Die Ah*."

THE ENGLISH

IT TOOK me seven years to master the rudiments of Singlish. It would take me seven lifetimes to understand Mancunian English. In hawker centres, Singaporeans converse in a relaxed fashion. But on the streets of Manchester, locals speak with a relaxed brain. It's very time-consuming. Casual greetings with strangers took so long that I often nipped away and grabbed a bite to eat, before returning to hear the rest of the sentence.

"Helloo, luuurrrvvvveeee," they would begin. "Ahhh yaaa, all-riiiiiight?" It was three days before: a) I realised I was being asked, "Hello love, are you all right?" And b) I shoved four Duracell batteries in their mouths to speed up vocal delivery. Officially, of course, I was in Manchester, in the freezing north-west of England in December 2002 to cover entertaining Premiership matches and, if I was free, to also watch Manchester United.

Unofficially, I was in Manchester to track down every loony, nutcase and space cadet that Lancashire had to offer. I've been working on this mission in Toa Payoh for several years now, but I never realised that my duties extended to northern England.

My first basket case found me while I waited at a bus stop in a Lancashire village called Worsley. The place is so quiet that the local council has been discussing shooting its duck population because residents have complained that the occasional quack has increased noise pollution by 45 per cent.

As you can see, the deranged elderly have a lot of time on their hands in Worsley. So, they like to while away the hours with the odd, impromptu mime class.

When I was at the bus stop, a bus pulled in, so I tilted my head to read its destination on the side. An old woman, who was sitting on the bus above the sign, smiled at me and then tilted her head. Slightly disturbed, I rolled my head towards my other shoulder and she did the same.

Safe in the knowledge that a bus separated me from the lunatic, I began moving my head backwards and forwards and she copied my every move. We looked like a pair of those cheap, nodding dogs people have on their shelves in Singapore. Then, demonstrating the first signs of spontaneity, the daft old bat started to wave at me vigorously and gave me a toothless grin. I've got more fingers than she had teeth.

Unfortunately, just as I contemplated asking the old dear to come and live with me, the bus pulled away. I was devastated. Priceless nutters like them can be so hard to find. Luckily, they find me. I went into a newsagent for directions to the nearest post office and regretted it instantly because only one of us was fluent in northern English.

"Helloo, luuurrrvvvveeee,"' said the shop owner. "Where? Aye. You wanna ge' a boose. It's tool fah t'wark."

"No, I don't mind walking." That was a mistake. Manchester only has two seasons — June and winter.

"Riiiiiight, aye. Tech the furs' riiiiiight. Goal pass the red paws box and yule see paws office next t'it."

After I'd gone through my English/northern English dictionary and translated her directions, she added: "Boot it worn be open now, luuurrrvvvveeee." I took one of the quacking ducks from the nearby canal and threw it at her.

Compared to Mancunian, Singlish really is a walk in the park. I'd forgotten, incidentally, that during those walks in the park, loonies do enjoy a heated argument with themselves.

Strolling through Manchester's Piccadilly Gardens in the city centre, I saw a rather intoxicated chap screaming abuse at his alter ego about that "fucking waste of space, Tony Blair".

Then in the next breath, Dr Jekyll replied: "But look how the Prime Minister's cleaned up this place."

This infuriated Mr Hyde, who retorted: "Nope, Tony Blair is a fucking Tory in a cheap Labour suit."

It was positively wonderful. My only regret was the old tramp didn't start fighting with himself. I would have brought in popcorn and charged admission for that.

The Singapore Tourism Board (STB) should pay his salary (a cheap bottle of cider and a urine-stained overcoat seems to make him extremely happy) and bring this man to Hong Lim's Speakers' Corner. Give him any issue you like — foreign talent, Medisave, ez-link cards, prescription chewing gum — and let him go to work. He doesn't need to read up on the subjects because from what I understand, facts merely cloud his judgement. Just give him plenty of room and a discreetly placed bucket. Both Jekyll and Hyde, unsurprisingly, have an acute bladder problem.

Indeed, if the STB is serious about providing quality street entertainment, then I suggest they secure his services now.

Because I've heard he shares a room in the asylum with a really good mime artist.

NOTE: I received a letter from an expat who had actually worked in the Manchester village of Worsley. Well, someone's got to I suppose.

THE CAMPAIGN

AFTER leaving my family behind in England, having spent Christmas and the New Year with them, I was rather depressed and needed cheering up. I'd just infuriated a Singaporean busload of impatient commuters by waving my old farecard at the ez-link card reader. Surprisingly, the machine wouldn't beep. Unsurprisingly, my uncensored language produced a few beeps of its own as I struggled to come to terms with the latest technological miracle of efficiency.

I'd only been away for five weeks, but it might as well have been five years. In the end, a teenager rather patronisingly explained that the farecard was now defunct and I had to use an ez-link card instead.

The embarrassing scene was reminiscent of the time I showed my grandmother how to use a VCR. "So you put the tape in like this, Nan," I told her, while performing the task in slow motion. "This slot is only for videotapes, okay? It's not a mailbox. This is the last time I'm getting the letters out, all right? Now, stop dribbling."

Back on the bus, I thanked the teenager with a discreet farecard paper-cut to his forearm and sulked all the way to the MRT station at Toa Payoh. And then, the dark clouds dissipated and sunlight filtered through my black mood.

The blinding light came in the form of an SMRT poster, which proudly announced the all-new Courtesy Awareness Campaign for 2003. The acronym is CAP, though I'm sure there should be an 'R' in there somewhere. Perceptively aware that commuters might, at this stage, gouge out their eyeballs to avoid reading the poster in its entirety, this campaign vowed to be "more fun and exciting".

Now, there is a quiz. That's right, there is an online quiz to determine whether you are a selfless angel or a *kiasu* bastard when travelling on Singaporean public transport. I couldn't wait to get home to participate.

In entertainment terms, the quiz might fall short of, say, *Who Wants To Be A Millionaire* or an irritable bowel, but it's an enlightening exercise nonetheless. I won't spoil the content for you, but let's just say the quiz writers are fond of pregnant women questions along the lines of: "If a pregnant lady goes into labour on a train, would you cut the umbilical cord and give up your seat for the newborn baby?"

If foreigners participate, they could be forgiven for thinking the MRT is full of nothing other than heavily pregnant women. As a precaution, SMRT should look into this and ensure that its drivers are all fully trained midwives. I'm only bitching because I scored a pitiful nine out of 16 and my scorecard read: "Kind, but could be kinder."

That's a rather cruel character assassination. I've secured seats for pregnant women on countless occasions by bundling little old ladies to the floor.

But Singapore loves a condescending campaign or two doesn't it? There have been campaigns for, among other things, courtesy on public transport, killer litter, cleaner toilets, feeding stray cats and picking your nose at family gatherings.

No, hang on, that last one came from my mother, not the Singapore government. There aren't any posters for that one and Gurmit Singh hasn't made any commercials for it. But my mother's campaign does come with a slap across the head, which has enjoyed considerable success over the years. Perhaps SMRT should adopt a similar approach.

The network's efforts to cultivate a more gracious and courteous commuter should be applauded, but will a poster and a quiz really transform the *kiasu* elements of this society? To be fair, having spent Christmas travelling on the crumbling, litter-strewn London Underground, one shouldn't be too hard on SMRT.

Besides, the airline industry is still 30,000 feet ahead when it comes to patronising its fellow passengers. Whether it was Changi or Heathrow, I still had to go through that pathetic 'terrorist' interrogation. A Changi Airport employee asked the same tired, old question: "Did anyone approach you to carry something through for them?"

Does she seriously expect me to reply: "Well, do you see that man over there; the one wearing the balaclava? He asked me to take through two souvenir M16s for him. I put them in my suitcase because they were too heavy for my hand luggage. Do I get extra air miles for that?"

Within six months, don't be surprised if Changi Airport unveils the "fun and exciting" Say No To Terrorists quiz, with questions like: "If someone asked you to carry a teddy bear in you luggage and it started ticking, what would you do?"

No one is disputing the threat of global terrorism since Sept 11. But airport officials asking such banal questions will not bring about the collapse of Al Qaeda. Hold that thought, while I pick my nose in peace. That's about the only public campaign that hasn't been launched in Singapore — yet.

NOTE: I remain deeply impressed with how many campaigns this country nurtures in a year. The originality really is quite staggering. They'll be campaigns on love and romance next...

THE ROMANCE

WHEN I was a teenager, I'd like to think young ladies were drawn to me at social gatherings. I made other men feel insecure in my presence. I was a bit of a sex magnet in fact. To visualise this scenario, however, I have to imagine that the only other males in the room were Mr. Bean, George Michael and Barney the dinosaur, but it's my imagination damn it and I'll go wherever it takes me.

But the dream never lasts long anyway. The bubble always bursts when the Michelle Pfeiffer-lookalike rips through my banter by declaring that she's seen *Jurassic Park* 12 times and she has an inexplicable fetish for the colour purple.

To be honest, I attracted about as many women as Singapore attracts opposition candidates at general elections. If only women could've been encouraged to like me. If there had been, say, a group of geeks who went around Dagenham, my hometown, ordering single people to get together, my chances would've improved tenfold. But who the hell would go to all that trouble to create a taskforce to promote romance and social couplings?

Stand up, Singapore, and proudly take one matchmaking step forward. In a bid to get more Singapore citizens to have sex (and, I presume, conceive babies to bolster the workforce in 20 years time), February 2003 was designated the month to be one of love, life and relationships. The lovemaking campaign — Romancing Singapore — was launched by the bigwigs. Sorry, I'm wrong. It isn't a campaign — of course it isn't, the Republic doesn't have campaigns — but a festival and celebration of love.

Don't reach for the sick bucket just yet; this celebration shouldn't involve hippies, peace symbols or Beatles songs. There will be no mimicking of Woodstock, with mass gatherings of sex-starved youths at Sentosa. But there is, however, a Task Force. The organisers, Family Matters! (with an exclamation no less), have spared no expense to ensure that Singaporeans celebrate their love for one another. So you'd better be bloody romantic in February or they'll send the Task Force troops in.

Some of Singapore's finest military men have been trained by social workers and are going into the combat zone armed with candles, flowers and copies of the international bestseller, *Save Your Marriage! Forget Barney, He's Not As Well Endowed As He Looks.*

If you're sitting in a cinema with a young dating couple beside you and they start bickering, resist the temptation to drown them in popcorn. Just wait five minutes for the Romancing Singapore Task Force to arrive and they'll do it for you. Armed with guns, knives and heart-shaped pillows, the sensitive soldiers will have the little domestic fracas resolved in no time.

Covering all the angles, naturally, the Task Force even has a website, www.romancingsingapore.com, which gives invaluable tips on how to be a romantic. Whether you are married, dating or single, there is something for everyone here.

Married couples, for instance, are encouraged to watch a midnight show, which I'm sure is a foolproof way of shoring up a drooping love life. After all, camcorders are relatively inexpensive these days so you just need to find space in the bedroom for the tripod.

Dating couples are encouraged to spend a night at a museum. Another inspired idea. Some of those displays are older than the fossils. A young couple could spend hours up there before they're discovered by the wheezing security guard.

Of course, there are liberal-minded cynics who'd claim this Task Force is yet another Orwellian example of third-party interference: A rather desperate, transparent attempt to get more people to have more sex, more of the time.

Well, all I can say is; where the hell was this Task Force when I was 16? I grew up on a council housing estate in Dagenham where there were only two residents NOT having sex — the church vicar and me. Where was my Greater London campaign to generate a fine romance or two?

I could make girls laugh at times. Sexy classmates often said: "Do you know, for an ugly beanpole, you're occasionally funny."

To which I replied: "That's bloody marvellous. But how many times does a girl have to laugh before she contemplates removing some underwear — preferably mine?"

I was usually slapped and deservedly so. But if there had been a romance Task Force at my side, things would've been different. My tormentor would've been severely reprimanded for disrupting our love vibes and punished for hindering any chances of a relationship. She'd feel humiliated, I'd bask in my minor triumph and the romance taskforce would march off to deal with the next crime of passion.

And then, the humbled girl would kick me in the testicles and walk off into the sunset — with the guy who had a nose like Barney.

NOTE: I received several emails from Singaporeans who were irritated by what they saw as yet another attempt by certain people to interfere in their private lives. If a woman is happily single, for instance, does she really need some ridiculous festival full of do-gooders making themselves busy and encouraging her to pair off with some soppy sod?

Can you imagine if it was sex-related? If any of these festival planners ever approached me and said: "Good afternoon, sir. We're from Romancing Singapore and we hear you're having problems getting it up?" I'd take his clipboard and shove it up his arse. That said, the festival continued unabashed across the country. For almost a month, advertisements were placed in newspapers and magazines giving patronising and largely useless tips on how to improve one's love life. It was stunningly pathetic and trivial. In the middle of a never-ending recession, you'd think the governing powers would have more pressing issues such as rising unemployment, political apathy, Islamic extremism and migrations to Australia. They shouldn't waste their time by telling single Singaporeans whether chocolates or flowers are more suitable on a first date. It's up to the individual. The busybodies should mind their own bloody business.

THE PYJAMAS

IT'S finally over. For a while there, it seemed like it would never end. No, I'm not referring to the recent budget speech, but the recent Romancing Singapore campaign/celebration/festival. From what I understand, prostate examinations are quicker and less painful.

If you recall, indeed I'm sure you'll never forget, the month of February 2003 will go down in Singapore history as the month of love, romance and a rather large helping of Singapore's all-girl band, *Cherry Chocolate Candy*. All of which was organised by the Singapore Task Force on behalf of Family Matters! And don't you dare forget that exclamation mark damn it!

There are website rumours that George Lucas is rewriting a key love scene in Episode III of *Star Wars*. Anakin Skywalker and Senator Amidala will exchange heart-shaped pillows and Obi-Wan Kenobi will utter the immortal line: "Remember, the Singapore Task Force will be with you, always."

But you certainly can't fault the Task Force for effort, can you? They spread out across the island like a battalion of love-makers organising everything from gentle river cruises under a starry, starry night to nostalgic drive-in movies.

The latter was a bit of a tragedy for me. I can't drive and, with hindsight, turning up on a BMX bicycle was probably a bad idea. It was a big turn-off for the ladies and I ended up with a sore groin. Moreover, the wicker basket at the front was, I suspect, a touch too feminine, hindering my chances of impressing all the pretty girls. But that particular activity was inspired compared to the late night pyjama party for singles, which was an unmitigated disaster.

Have you seen a grown man in nothing but a pair of stripy pyjamas? He looks about as sexually desirable as, well, a grown man in a pair of stripy pyjamas. Slumber parties are for teenaged girls to eat popcorn and gossip wistfully about handsome teenaged boys. Or in Dagenham, where I grew up, all night parties were for teenaged boys to discover pornography and recognise the importance of being well endowed.

A skinny adult, however, in stripy pyjamas looks like a giant blob of toothpaste. Would you invite Mr. Aquafresh into your bedroom? According to media reports, only one man turned up appropriately attired at the campaign's pyjama party. He is my hero. He should be the next Singaporean president. In fact, he should be the next Singaporean president in stripy pyjamas. If Mr. Aquafresh doesn't impress foreign dignitaries then no one will. By all accounts, my hero wasn't inhibited at the party, but he took the precaution of sewing up his frontal flap first. He was a little disturbed, perhaps, but he didn't want to come across as dangerous.

But the post-puberty pyjama party was not as baffling as the festival's obsession with the beach. First, there was the kissing competition at the Pasir Ris beach. Now I'm not bitching because the organisers turned down my request to be both judge and demonstrator, but why pick the beach for a snogging contest? If I threw 50kg of salt onto a damp floor, would you lay down with your partner and start eating each other?

But it didn't end there. On the Romancing Singapore website, (there is always, always a website) there were several polls, loosely related to shagging. There was one question that asked: Which was the romantic beach in Singapore: East Coast, Pasir Ris, Changi Point or Sentosa? The actual answer should be of course, none of the above. Has the Singapore Task Force of love-makers never stepped on a beach? We smother ourselves in tanning creams, get sun burnt, then the wind blows, the sand gets stuck to our skin and we spend the rest of the day looking like a jam doughnut. Would you invite Mr. Jam Doughnut into your bedroom?

The one glaring omission from the website's plethora of romantic questions was: Who would you rather date Mr. Aquafresh or Mr. Jam Doughnut? But the Task Force was relentless. Even commuters on the No. 65 bus were not spared the message of love and sex. In the middle of February, *Cherry Chocolate Candy* jumped aboard and gave away free CDs of love songs. Bewildered aunties were heard to ask: "You Cherry Chocolate wha'? Got free ice cream is it? Got sample or not?"

This wasn't such a big deal to me. Where I grew up, many of the old drunks in east London wouldn't have been too impressed with *Cherry Chocolate Candy*. Having staggered onto the last night bus after the pubs had closed, they think they see beautiful women bearing gifts every night. Of course, what they actually see is a woman in blue, bearing a breathalyser.

But now that the hilarity has subsided and the rip-roaring activities have concluded, the campaign/festival/celebration/

baby-making exercise has come to a sad end.

A colleague in the office said it was a noble plan that was poorly executed. No, it wasn't. That's grossly unfair on the volunteers and organisers who genuinely worked hard throughout February to make the festival a success for many people across Singapore.

On the contrary, Romancing Singapore was a poor plan that was nobly executed. The campaign's intentions were hardly honourable. This was top-down cynicism at its worst.

What sort of festival or campaign can we expect next? A free savings account with every pregnancy? A $1,000 discount, per baby, off the latest Space Wagon? A nationwide ban on contraception? Perhaps Aquafresh and Jam Doughnut could form a singing duo and re-release that Guns And Roses classic, *Sweet child of mine. Let's make babies all the time.*

But that would be ludicrous, wouldn't it? And yet, an anal civil servant desperate to reach the next rung on the bureaucratic ladder, could be reading this right now and thinking: "That song has a catchy lyric. It might just work. I mean, if we can get grown men to wear pyjamas..."

THE HOOKERS

"WE'RE coming to Singapore," she said. "I've been on the Internet and I've found some hotels and they're really cheap. You told me Singaporean hotels were expensive, but these are much cheaper than anything in London. With a bit of saving, we could easily afford these prices." My mother was so excited. It had been five years since I moved to Singapore and she hadn't yet visited. But, according to her, that was about to change.

"These hotels are budget hotels, but that's all right. We're not snobs, are we? They're near to buses and trains apparently and not that far from that place, Orchard Road, where the shops and restaurants are."

"That sounds great, mum," I replied, rather enthusiastically, over the phone. "Where are they?"

"In some place called 'Gay-lang'. There's a chain of them called Hotel 81. They say it's a lively area."

"It certainly is a lively place."

"Yeah? Will there be things for your step-dad to do there? To keep him busy?"

"Oh, absolutely."

"What about your little brother?"

"I bloody hope not mum, it's the red light district."

"What? You mean prostitutes?... Fucking hell... We won't bloody stay there then."

"Fair enough, mum."

"What sort of place is this Singapore? You said it was clean and safe and you can't eat chewing gum. Now you're telling me the place is full of old tarts with all their bits hanging out on street corners?"

"Yes, mum."

"What about little Gary then, eh? You think I can let your little brother walk about when there's all these tarts all over the place?"

"No, mum."

"No, mum is bloody right. We'll spend a fortnight down in Ramsgate instead. I mean, I know we have to put up with the smell of horse shit from the stables next door, but at least your little brother can go out on his bike in peace. And I won't have to worry about him bumping into some old tart's tits."

"Fair enough, mum."

Sometimes I wish I hadn't told her. I can imagine my mother, who's not one to keep her opinions to herself, expressing concern at the number of women standing in line along the streets.

"This is terrible. Singaporeans aren't too bloody bright are they? I've only been here for five minutes and I know that the bus stop is further down the road. I'd better go and sort them out... Excuse me... the bus stop is up there. The buses won't stop here... I'm sorry?... Fifty dollars for what?... Here, there's no need to be so bloody rude. I should wash your mouth out with soap and water if I were you."

But the world's oldest profession continues to thrive in Singapore. I've been down to Geylang's red-light district several times because there are some decent coffee shops in the area. Well, that's my story and I'm sticking to it. My old friend David, who was the first Singaporean I met, took me to the various houses of ill repute during my first week on the island. It was a novelty, at first, because women wanted me. Usually, they don't. But in Geylang, a tall Caucasian seems to suggest a rather large wallet. So the compliments came thick and fast. I was frequently asked "Hey handsome (pronounced 'ham-sum'), you want a good time?" Or "Hey, big boy, come inside." Curiously, I've been called 'big boy' on numerous occasions in Singapore, sometimes by old uncles. It's most flattering, but also, a trifle disturbing.

I know the ladies of the night only wanted the money they assumed I had, but I lapped up the attention nonetheless. Call me fickle and shallow, but in 28 years I've perfected the art of repulsing women. To be sure, many men say this, usually in a transparent attempt to appear sensitive in an 'aw-shucks' kind of way. But I can honestly say it's the truth. Indeed, I actually achieved the impossible with the opposite sex — British prostitutes turned me down and it was their job to say yes.

When I was studying in Manchester, part of our post-pub drunken routine was to tease hookers by asking for the price list. "How much will a shag cost?" we'd ask, before roaring with laughter.

"Fuck off, you student wankers. You ain't got no fucking money," came the humbling, but truthful reply.

Along the streets of Geylang, however, I was treated like a white god. Like respectful tourists, we walked along the seedier streets, peering into the dimly lit living rooms that served as brothels and then we left and had a *prata* supper.

But that wasn't the end of it. Years later, some colleagues and I went back to Geylang's mean streets out of curiosity. This trip wasn't fun, however, it was horrifying. Watching young girls sell their bodies at 3am was deeply disturbing for me. My parents divorced when I was four years old, so I grew up in a house with two wonderful, hard-working women. In 20 years, both my mother and sister taught me more about feminism than any pretentious textbook or patronising, middle-class sociologist ever could. Consequently, I never had the inclination to discuss prostitution in Singapore. It's been done before and has become a tedious cliché in itself. Besides, I've always argued that, despite the assumptions of other western writers, there is so much more to Singapore than Sarong Party Girls chasing rich white men and hookers chasing any men. That belief still holds. Yet I can't deny that prostitution eats away at this society like a stubborn tumour that simply refuses to go away.

A little research discovered that there are around 400 brothels in Singapore. Yes, that's 400. To be fair, I'm sure that figure wasn't arrived at via a comprehensive survey. If anything, the statistic could be higher. If you are the proprietor of a number of illicit brothels, you're probably not in a great hurry to register your business, are you? But still, for a country smaller than greater London, that's a lot of hookers. Apparently, there are something like 10 to 20 prostitutes in each brothel, which means dirty old men have approximately 6,000 women to choose from.

You won't find photographs of these ladies in the Singapore Tourism Board's *Things To Do In Singapore* guide, of course. But everybody knows where they are. What I didn't realise was that these places are not just ad hoc meat racks established in various nooks and crannies. These brothels operate in geo-graphically, and legally, defined districts of Singapore. They are termed designated red-light areas (DRA's). Only a Singaporean civil servant could come up with the term 'designated red-light areas' and not laugh.

In England, hookers operated in areas known as NFPA, which stood for No Fucking Policemen Around. But prostitution was never as organised, much less legalised, as it is in Singapore. It's so systematic it's terrifying. Hookers must carry a yellow health card at all times, which can only be earned through regular hospital check ups. In London, a quick post-pub nightcap with a Soho 'working girl' and you risked catching 'the clap', which is a wonderfully romantic colloquialism for a sexually transmitted disease. No chance of that in Singapore.

The commonly known DRA's, and I'm sure there are others, are Desker Road, Orchard Road's Orchard Towers, which is tastefully known as the four floors of whores and, of course, Geylang. Home to some great hawker centres, thousands of foreign workers and countless brothels, Geylang serves Singa-poreans in the same way that Soho serves Londoners. It's a haven for the sex-starved. I've been there several times with friends and we laugh, ogle and make predictable, juvenile comments, male banter and all that bullshit. But honestly, the place is a public sewer. You end up feeling like Robert De Niro's deranged *Taxi Driver*, praying that torrential rain will wash away the sleazy clientele and blow the nocturnal nightmare from the memory.

I've encountered prostitution before, of course. I'm not going to pretend I was Dagenham's answer to The Artful Dodger, but I did come across one or two stone-faced ladies selling their wares in Manchester's city centre late at night, when I was there as a student. But I never felt sympathy for them in the same way that I do for the young girls in Geylang. In Manchester, and this will sound grossly stereotypical I know, the women were so typically fierce and resilient. Hard as nails, they could humiliate you in front of your peers with one savage tongue lashing. Metaphorically, of course, not literally. Undoubtedly, that may have been a facade. No one wants to be standing on Manchester's Oxford Road at 1am, trying to somehow make a frozen body look sexually desirable. Nevertheless, if their ferocious independence was an act, it was pretty damn convincing.

In Geylang, the poor girls look so young and fragile, you want to rescue them like some patronising Victorian liberal. You certainly don't want to sleep with them. Many of the girls are from China, of course, and I'm aware of the scheming Chinese "Crows" who arrive here to work these Singaporean streets paved with gold. Perhaps the girls I've seen, standing outside seedy hotels at 3am, are merely keeping up appearances too. Perhaps, their demure, innocent, slightly startled look is all an act too. But if they really are heartless, ruthless money grabbers then they, too, are pretty damn convincing.

I've watched Geylang girls, still in their teens, smile weakly as disgusting middle-aged uncles, wearing sweaty vests and dirty flip-flops, haggle over the price. Small groups of men gather round to discuss the merits of each prostitute, providing heartwarming critiques of each girl such as: "That one not bad, ah? She look so young one. Like schoolgirl. But her chest so lousy, she got nothing what. Forget it lah, that one not worth 50 bucks."

The Dickensian scene reminded me of a British movie called *Mona Lisa*, where actor Bob Hoskins trawls London's underworld of crime and prostitution. Ironically, you cannot buy this classic movie in Singapore, uncensored at least, because it contains one or two tame sex scenes. But not to worry, you can get the real deal for less than the price of a DVD down at Geylang anyway. The hypocrisy is stunning.

Singapore sells itself, if you'll pardon the pun, to its citizens, to foreign talent and to tourists as one of the safest, cleanest and most wholesome countries on the planet. And in many respects, it is. But if you cut through the government's rhetoric and slice open the society's underbelly, you'll find 18-year-old girls wearing too much make up telling 50-year-old men that oral sex and full intercourse can be arranged, as long as the price is right. Or perhaps you'll discover the skeletal, chain-smoking, pockmarked pimps hovering around the hookers at a safe distance. Supposedly, there are no pimps, like there are no street walkers. But a nod and a wink to the greasy man with tattoos standing in the background and you've got yourself a cheap, but not free, date for a couple of hours.

But we can't go down that road because, apparently, it doesn't exist. At election rallies or during National Day speeches, when was the last time you heard a politician say: "We must continue to tighten our belts. I know we said that last year and the year before, and the year before. But you all must be losing weight, from all those extra, unpaid hours, not to mention the lunch breaks you keep missing, so there's still one more notch left on your belt. So we can squeeze a little more, before you either burst or emigrate to Australia. We have no choice. Banking and finance is down 4 per cent, thanks to China. The electronics sector is down 13 per cent, thanks to China. And manufacturing is down 28 per cent, thanks to China. Fortunately, the hooker industry experienced a 4 per cent growth in 2003, thanks to

China. Those desperate girls are so much cheaper than those in Southeast Asia. Keep up the good work, girls!"

You haven't, because society chooses to close an eye to the various DRA's. Besides, according to a popular stereotype, these brothels are there to service the thousands of sex-starved foreign, construction workers living on the island. That's certainly true. But they have to wait their turn, along with the Chinese, Malay, Indian and Eurasian Singaporeans that I've seen hovering around the prostitutes. And did I mention the *ang mohs*? Both the so-called foreign talents and the western tourists. Without their wallets, Orchard Road's four floors of whores would have been downsized years ago.

And Desker Road, which appeared to be the seediest and cheapest DRA, enjoys the company of a Caucasian or two in the twilight hours. Of course, Desker Road is unlikely to be referred to on the news, in current affairs programmes or on welcoming posters at Changi Airport. The next time you arrive at Terminal One, don't expect a poster that says: "Welcome to Singapore. Get a tan at Sentosa. Get laid at Desker Road." It should, therefore, come as no surprise that I actually discovered Desker Road after a visiting friend from London told me about it. I'd vaguely heard of local friends joke about the place, of course. But my travelling Londoner knew that the street was popular with transvestites, 'lady-boys' and hookers who've had sex change operations. He was aware that this particular DRA boasted some of the lowest prices in Singapore, but the services were not as reputable or as clinical perhaps as Orchard Towers or Geylang.

How did he know all of this? From a British-made travel documentary, hosted by Lily Savage, a popular drag queen in Britain. Taking an off-beat, underground route, Savage pokes fun at the seedier side of Singaporean life. I'm told the documentary is very funny. But would it be shown here? Would a similar travel show be made by a Singaporean production team here? What do you think? Outsiders, some 10,000 km away, are allowed to know what really goes on in this tiny city-state in the small hours, but don't expect Singaporeans to be allowed to watch such a show. They only live here. I'm sure most Singaporeans are not interested in the more sordid aspects of their culture. But they should at least have the choice.

If nothing else, paying a visit to Desker Road, gave me the chance to see the finest pair of breasts I'd ever seen. Listening to my guest explain, in disturbing detail, every aspect of Desker Road's services, curiosity got the better of me so we persuaded my old Singaporean friend, David, to be our chauffeur for the evening. Driving along the street at 4am while it was raining was probably not the most astute decision we'd ever made. Desker Road looked about as exciting as an HDB void deck at 4am. Short on customers, the few call girls who had braved the monsoon conditions were undoubtedly aware of the situation and sought to liven up proceedings. Driving past slowly in the car, a young woman walked over and flashed her breasts at us. There's no need for gory details. But, suffice it to say, my friend grabbed my arm and shouted: "Fucking hell, did you see that? That was, without doubt, the greatest pair of tits I've ever seen. Did you see 'em, Neil? Fucking hell. They were perfect. Just perfect. Dave, Dave, turn around so we can see them again. You got to see them. What a fucking pair."

We did turn around. The breasts were once again exposed and, this time, David and I saw what all the fuss was about. The chest was indeed flawless. The only drawback was the boobs belonged to a man. A minor detail that David and I felt necessary to point out to our travelling friend.

"What? That can't be right. They were the greatest pair of knockers I've ever seen," he replied.

"Well, of course," I explained. "If you're going to have cosmetic surgery, you might as well get the most for your money right? It's very common around Orchard Towers too. I've seen quite a few around there. They're easy to spot after a while. Your documentary didn't teach you that, did it?"

"Fuck the documentary. I'm just glad you two are here. I might have shagged him otherwise. What a waste of a great pair of tits."

No arguments there. But at least my tourist friend knew where to find them. I didn't. And I'd been in Singapore for over four years before I went on my first, and only, excursion to Desker Road. I've got better things to do with my time than watch 50-year-old *ang mohs* discussing terms with a group of 'ladyboys' at 3am. I'm sure you do too. But that doesn't mean we should gloss over prostitution in Singapore and pretend it isn't there, in the same way many people ignore blind tissue-paper sellers or abused maids.

Think about it. There are more teenaged hookers in Geylang than there are Stamford Raffles statues in Singapore, but you won't see any 'ladyboys' on the cover of tourist brochures. Perhaps the Singapore Tourism Board should look into this. It is keen to provide visitors with a more enriching, cultural experience, which is more realistic and less superficial than the usual tours of famous colonial sites. And I'm sure more HDB dwellers have been to a Geylang hotel than Raffles Hotel.

In some ways, it would have been entertaining had my

family opted for that cheap hotel in Geylang's red-light district. My step-dad would've had women all over him like a rash. He'll claim this is nothing new to him, though he'd be secretly tickled by all the attention. But I'm sure the novelty would wear off. It did for me. When a Chinese hooker, who should still be in school, comes up and says: "Hey, you want blow job? Only 50 dollars. Or 80 dollars for you and your friend together," you feel like a US Marine in a bad Vietnam movie. And you feel sick. Because there's nothing funny about the situation at all, is there?

THE ACRONYMS

SINGAPORE'S hip-swingers have renamed Holland Village. I spoke to a 'trendy' friend who suggested a trip to the recently renovated haven of coffee shops, bars and bistros. What he actually said was: "Hey, let's check out Holland V."

To which I replied: "What the hell is Holland V, you stupid man?"

The only *V* I knew was a cult, science fiction TV show that I watched as a child in the '80s. If I recall correctly, the *V* stood for visitors — the unwanted extraterrestrial kind, not the Inland Revenue variety.

I therefore assumed that 'Holland V' was the sequel, where Dutch aliens turned up in clogs, handing out tulips and hookers from Amsterdam. But seriously, many Singaporeans are certainly fond of the odd acronym or six aren't they?

When I first arrived, a receptionist in my office would ask cheekily: "Are you an SPG fan or an S-N-A-G?"

My reply that I was, in fact, a Sagittarian never pacified her. Indeed, it merely aroused her curiosity further. "So which is it?" she would continue, "An SPG fan or an S-N-A-G?"

"Look, stop throwing letters at me. This isn't bloody Sesame Street."

But that was the overbearing first impression for me. The Republic must have been instructed to speak in acronyms, a doublespeak-like code from the novel *1984.* The powers that be must have declared in 1965: "We hereby proclaim Singapore an independent state and from this day on you will speak only in short forms, abbreviations and initials, preferably TLA's (three letter acronyms), so we can confuse our regional neighbours and antagonise the British, who pissed off during World War II and returned 50 years later wearing knee-high white socks with sandals."

When I was living in England, the only TLA I heard in my house was 'HRT', which was usually uttered by my mother through gritted teeth. I had no idea what HRT meant, but its mention was often preceded by frequent swearing and complaints about those "fucking doctors".

In Singapore, however, acronym-ese is another language altogether. If you can't converse like a dyslexic rapper, you'll soon get left behind. For example, last weekend, I went with a friend, who's a CEO, in his car to the SIR to get my EP to take to the HDB, via the MRT, using the card they call E-Z, then on to JB, along the BKE, for a cheap DVD.

Doesn't it all sound a little punch-me-in-the-face-and-cut-out-my-windpipe annoying? Forget Eminem and his gangsta rhymes. If Americans can produce the rapper's movie, *8 Mile,* then Singaporean filmmakers should get a camera crew down to the hawker centres and shoot *Lorong 8,* with fast-talking uncles spouting acronyms.

Even national newspapers resort to countless short forms

in their stories. Take the recent 24-hour child-care scandal, for instance. Rather than write out, in full, that the infamous child-care centre operates around the clock, newspapers settled for "24/7" instead. That's almost as lazy as the parents who sentenced their innocent children to the pre-school prison in the first place. Besides, the short form is incorrect. It should read "24/7 4 U BASTARDS."

Of course, the quirky aspects of any language can be titillating. My eccentric grandmother, whose vocabulary was complete before World War II and hasn't been expanded since, has a fondness for questioning my sexuality. When I visit, she looks concerned and says: "You know, you're looking ever so queer."

My nan, bless her, thinks she is expressing concern for my welfare. But in modern parlance, she is suggesting I have the physical characteristics of a fine homosexual.

But these short forms and abbreviations, on the other hand, are not amusing; they're irritating and often overused in a desperate attempt to sound cool.

Teenagers in my block tell me that they've hung out at "Macs" or "BK", as if they lack the breathing apparatus required to finish the sentence using gigantic, exhausting words such as McDonald's and Burger King.

Is the pace of the Singaporean ratrace now so fast that we lack the time to speak in full sentences? Instead, we have to converse in nonsensical gobbledegook that wouldn't look out of place in a Lewis Carroll novel.

Be careful, though. In a desperate attempt to prove they are *au fait* with Singaporean culture, bewildered expats will adopt the acronym jargon to show they have truly assimilated.

A Canadian friend once told me he'd had a great night down at "BQ". The idiot, of course, meant Boat Quay. This tickled me because in England, "B and Q" is a hardware store. You'd struggle to find an SPG there, but Caucasians with a screw loose are most welcome at both places. So let's tighten those screws before it's too late.

The next time a loony asks you to check out 'Holland V', 'Orchard R' or even 'Raffles P', give them a gentle slap and say: "URA ****". Oh, just use your imagination.

NOTE: Writing about the seemingly harmless topic of acronyms and short forms triggered an unexpected response. A rather self-satisfied, smug expat (and Singapore's not short on those, is it?) wrote to criticise my description of acronyms and abbreviations and proceeded to highlight in remarkable detail what constitutes an acronym, a short form and so on, all of which spectacularly missed the point. She seemed determined to put this working-class ruffian in his place and I'm sure it gave her something to boast about to her pals around the swimming pool at the condo. From more rational Singaporeans, however, I received some great responses. A frustrated father complained that he had just attended a parents' evening at his child's school and the teachers had spoken in confusing, unexplained acronyms and abbreviations all night long. He wanted to know what kind of message that was sending to the pupils. The bloody wrong one, we both agreed. *TODAY* published his letter and then the school replied the following day. It was hilarious. Not only was the letter appallingly written, which served only to further undermine the school, but it, too, missed the point. Instead, the principal droned on about how it was important to allow pupils to express themselves freely in class, ignoring the fact that they sound like spoon-fed robots when they just lazily regurgitate initials and short forms. Where's the originality in that? All I can say is there will be those in society who will miss the point from time to time and I do sympathise. So allow me to explain, "URA twat."

THE THIEF

WITHOUT wishing to sound flippant, Singaporean detectives have had the easiest policing job since Sergeant Jim Bergerac. Good old Bergerac, you see, was a fictional detective on a popular BBC drama, called *Bergerac*, which ran for 12 years from 1981. Within 60 minutes, the copper always got his man. Not through deduction, forensic science or even bribery (which is quite popular in Southeast Asia), but through geography.

The sleuth plied his trade in Jersey, one of the Channel Islands off the southern coast of England. Now, this island is a gigantic nine miles wide and five miles deep. If I recall correctly, Jim Bergerac would tick off the local sheep population from his list of suspects, thus leaving 14 people, three dogs and a couple of stray cats that swam over from Guernsey. Having deduced who the bad guy is, there would be a 30-second car chase just to get the ball rolling and prevent viewers from switching over to watch *The A-Team*. Then, Bergerac would get out of his car, have a croissant and wait for the villain to complete one round of the tiny island, before arresting him on the way back. Variations of this plot were repeated for 12 torturous years, which says more about the average British TV viewer than it does about the charismatic qualities of Jim Bergerac.

But the efficiency of Jersey's Colombo came back to me when I read a heartwarming report over the Chinese New Year holidays. On the first day of the Lunar New Year, four scumbags snatched around $1,300 in *hongbao* money from a mother in Yishun. The poor woman was with her daughter and the pair was on their way to visit relatives, but still she wasn't spared.

Within the hour, however, the four thieves had been caught at a nearby HDB block. Yes, that's within the hour. Now, I'm not sure if Bergerac serves as an adviser to the Singaporean police force, but I'd love to think his technique was at work. Apparently, one or two officers questioned the staff sergeant in charge of the very short case.

"But sir, if they've made off on foot, they could be halfway to Woodlands by now," said the youngest and most eager police officer.

"Relax, I've got more experience than you. I've been working in the heartlands for 20 years and I've got every episode of Bergerac on video. The blur buggers will just run around the block. You see, here they come now, all sweaty and out of breath. Be a good chap, will you? Stretch out your arm and grab the little bastards."

The four culprits were swiftly apprehended and, would you believe it, charged in court the following day. Now that's what I call justice. Like Jersey, Singapore has certainly benefitted from being small when it comes to policing the island. There can't be too many criminal safe houses in Yishun.

Having said that, success can't altogether be attributed to the Bergerac School for Small-Town Law Enforcers. When I was

17, I was mugged in a McDonald's in east London at knifepoint as two police officers sat in a patrol car OUTSIDE the restaurant. While I handed over the cash, I prayed that the two coppers would look up, ascertain the situation and beat the shit out of the young offenders. Instead, they did nothing except expand their waistlines with a Big Mac. Had the muggers run out to the patrol car brandishing their knives and their ill-gotten gains while singing *I Shot the Sheriff*, the bloody boys in blue would have done nothing. Except move on to their French fries perhaps.

Can you imagine those two at the scene of the crime in Yishun? The distraught woman would run up and scream: "Those four guys have stolen my *hongbao* money!"

"Your hong what?"

"Never mind. Never mind. Quick, it's those big guys there."

"Those Big Macs where? Hey, that's near the McDonald's. Come on, I haven't eaten for four minutes."

"But what about my money? I don't have any money."

"Now look, don't worry about that, madam. As it's Chinese New Year, we'll treat you this time. But you're only getting a Happy Meal. Is that alright?"

They would be utterly useless. In stark contrast, Singapore's public services have been in fine form over the festive period. Aside from police officers catching thieves in record time, the Singapore Civil Defence Force had a raging fire at the Thomson Road flower nurseries under control within 20 minutes on the second day of Chinese New Year. They had to fight through not only leaping flames, but also *kaypoh* drivers who stopped their cars to watch the blaze. I know many Singaporeans enjoy the odd firecracker or two to bring in the Lunar New Year, but this was ridiculous. And yet, despite these hazards, the SCDF tamed Thomson's towering inferno without suffering a single casualty or injury. Having lived with a younger sister who enjoyed setting fire to our kitchen periodically, I can only salute the Force's achievement. To be fair, they were never greeted by the sight of a seven-year-old girl standing in the middle of a sizeable fire and saying: "Well, what do you think? It's much bigger than the last one, isn't it?"

But their effort was impressive nonetheless. While most of the country has spent the weekend counting *hongbaos* and *mahjong* tiles, those guys have been out there salvaging *hongbaos* and half of Thomson Road. It's been a stirring start to the Year of the Goat so remember this ancient Chinese proverb: "When a thief steals your money in an HDB estate, let him run around the block first — and then kick the little shit in the balls when he comes back."

THE CYCLISTS

THE Singapore Police Force has publicly put its foot down. In response to a number of shocking stories and letters in national newspapers recently, the Force has boldly declared that selfish cyclists found cycling on pavements can be fined $20. Now the governing powers of Singapore have often been criticised for their rather eccentric laws, but this really is a Draconian bridge too far. A $20 fine just for riding on the pavement? What kind of law is that? Cyclists who harass law-abiding pedestrians should be strung up by their dangly bits, preferably with piano wire, and summarily executed. That's the only way Singapore is going to rid itself of the scourge of humanity. As far as I'm concerned, pavement-riding cyclists rank just below serial killers, but just above Romancing Singapore campaigners.

Incidentally, if one more TV commercial tells me I must find a partner, buy her flowers, kiss her passionately and produce lots of Singaporean babies then I will end up in court charged with 'killer TV litter'. But it's these *kiasu* riders that are currently proving to be the bigger menace.

There was a story recently that a poor woman was flagging down a bus at a bus stop and was knocked down by a speeding cyclist. She ended up with a cracked leg bone, a year-long limp and $10,000 in medical bills.

In Bukit Batok, a heavily pregnant woman tripped and fell after making a desperate attempt to avoid a cyclist who was riding like a deranged maniac behind her, according to an eyewitness.

I have the deepest sympathy for these victims. The lift doors have often opened at my HDB block and I've had to jump back to allow Evel Knievel to whiz past. There's never a plank of wood, or a blunderbuss, around when you want one is there?

The lazy cyclist, and motorcyclist for that matter, exemplifies the *kiasu* traveller in every sense, cutting corners both literally and metaphorically.

Behind my block in Toa Payoh is a narrow pedestrian crossing beneath the Pan Island Expressway that allows people to get to the bus stops in Thomson Road. Concrete bollards have been erected to deter cyclists. But that's not enough to deter these gormless erections, is it? Consequently, *kiasu* cyclists and motor-cyclists, eager to bypass the pillars, have created four paths on the adjacent grass patch, so they now have a ready shortcut instead of having to go all the way around Lorong 1 to reach Thomson Road.

Morons on magnificent motorbikes have tooted the horn at me several times to get out of the way. But I've usually relied on my horn to remind the bugger who has the right of way. In extreme cases of persistent overtaking, I've tried to pursue the rider to kick him in his horn but alas, I've yet to hit the target.

Now, my girlfriend and I have created a little dance that we do as we walk along the footpath. Whenever a motorcyclist revs

Scribbles from the Same Island

up behind us, we continually move in the same direction as the bike to prevent any overtaking, singing: "To the left. And to the right. Keep it going, keep it going. It's all right."

I've warned my girlfriend not to do this when she is alone for fear of antagonising the impatient cyclist. The joke could turn quite nasty. And, alas, it did — for the motorcyclist.

One morning, an annoying little bastard kept his hand on his horn, one that emitted high-pitched sounds, all the way down the path, forcing irritated pedestrians to throw themselves against the fence to allow the bugger to pass. Reluctantly, my girlfriend also let him pass, otherwise, knowing her, he could still be there with her jumping in the same direction as the bike and refusing to let him pass.

Just a couple of seconds after riding around my missus, though, the prick attempted to overtake two schoolgirls, but his handlebars clipped the fence and he fell over the top of his motorbike. According to biased reports from my girlfriend, it was marvellous.

Clearly unruffled by the incident, she approached the fallen rider, stepped over him and continued to the bus stop as if nothing had happened. Priceless. But where did these people come from? What kind of sphincter is so impatient that he must overtake two schoolchildren on a motorbike on a public footpath?

When I was a kid all we had to worry about as junior pedestrians was being knocked over by shortsighted old ladies driving motorised vehicles. Without their mini cars, these people were passive, adorable old aged pensioners. Behind the wheel, they became geriatric Michael Schumachers shouting things like: "Take that, you little bastard. That's the last time you kick your ball into my front garden."

At a supermarket one Saturday morning, I swear I heard one pensioner saying to another: "I only got two this morning, Rose. I got that little bastard at number 21 who keeps stealing my pints of milk. And I got that Humphreys boy at number 15 who giggles at my blue-rinse hairdo."

Generally speaking, though, we tolerated the elderly's motorised deathtraps because they suffered a World War and Cliff Richard records for us. But I would watch *Summer Holiday* endlessly before I'd move aside for some impatient, tooting motorcyclist behind me. So the only solution is this — shoot the bastards. And I'm sure those crow killers would dutifully oblige. I once saw them gleefully massacre a family of crows in Toa Payoh Central, so they seem the trigger-happy type. They could hide under the tree to shoot crows and then they could hide in the tree to take aim at reckless cyclists. Proudly wearing those luminous, government-issued sashes, they could be Singapore's first official crow/cyclist shooters — licensed to kill parasites.

Any crow found stealing a chicken wing from a table at a hawker centre: the death penalty. Any motorcyclist found overtaking schoolgirls on a pedestrian footpath: the death penalty. Alternatively, the Singapore Police Force could pay me $20 and I will gladly hide at the Thomson Road pedestrian crossing and shove a branch into the spokes of every passing motorcycle.

NOTE: It is nigh on impossible to predict which topic or subject will evoke public reaction. But I can honestly say that the seemingly harmless topic of selfish, impatient cyclists would not have been at the top of my list. Not for the first time, I was proved to be utterly incorrect. Dedicated cyclists were rather miffed by my criticisms. One particular writer said I should experience the sufferings of the leisure cyclist over at the East Coast Park, before I make such accusations. I have, many times, and he is right. Roads designated for cyclists are constantly being swamped by joggers, dog-walkers and skateboarders. And, when you think about it, in the interest of fairness, there's only one solution to that problem, isn't there? They should be shot, too. In Singapore, god knows it's difficult enough for anyone to find a bit of space to themselves. In an island so desperately scarce in land, anyone who invades the personal space of another, whatever the circumstances or vehicle, is a bit of a selfish bastard when you think about it. Now, where's my bloody gun?

THE FAMILY

MY mother just called to tell me she's back safely from the hospital. She was there for a pre-op checkup. She's having a trapped nerve in her hand fixed. As always, there was a story to tell. When she went into the nurse's room, she was shocked to learn that she had to strip for a number of routine tests. This caused a bit of apprehension. Firstly, my mother is rather self-conscious. Like most people, she's not one for prancing around in a nurse's room with exposed genitalia. Secondly, she hadn't shaved her legs that day and had, in her words, "legs like a fucking Italian footballer." To top it off, she wore a pair of my stepdad's white, toweling sports socks. According to her, she looked "fucking awful".

Understandably, she got a little worked up, which forced her blood pressure to go through the roof, which in turn made her more worked up and so on. As a result, the wonderfully patient nurse couldn't get an accurate reading from her stressed patient. So the nurse said: "I know what's wrong here, Sue, you're a bit nervous aren't you love?"

"Well, yeah, I am a bit," replied my poor mother. "I don't do this sort of thing very often."

"Is it the nakedness that's making you nervous, dear?"

"Well, yeah, it is a bit uncomfortable."

"Don't worry, love, we'll soon fix that." And with that, she whipped off the top half of her nurses' uniform. Please, allow me to say that again. She whipped off the top half of her bloody nurses' uniform. The middle-aged woman stood there in a bra that could have housed a small family in each cup. Don't think sexy soft pornography here. Think Carry On Middle-Aged Matron Who Should Know Better. Suddenly, the Italian footballer's legs and Andre Agassi socks didn't seem to concern my poleaxed mother. Headlines like "Teaching Assistant Suffers Deranged Lesbian Attack In Hospital" occupied her thoughts instead.

"Does that make you feel a bit better now, Sue? A little less awkward perhaps?" The kind, but semi-naked, nurse asked.

"Oh, yeah. Thanks." My mother lied. Speaking on the phone shortly after the visit, my mother told me: "The next time I go back, I'm going to make sure my pulse and blood pressure are so low, they'll think I'm dead. I can't have that bloody nurse getting her tits out again."

I really miss my mother. That was my way of telling you that. I came off the phone with tears in my eyes and a stomachache. No one can make me laugh like my loopy family. Telephone calls like that always give me a slight pang of homesickness. Not for the country, you understand. I don't get homesick for any country. Flag-waving patriotism is best left behind in Hitler's bunker. But I miss my family terribly. And despite what anybody living overseas may tell you, it never gets easier.

In late 1996, when I was 21, my mother kicked me up the arse, threw my suitcase at me and said: "Right, now fuck off. And don't come back until you've seen a bit of the world." One of her regrets when she was younger was that her poor, working-class upbringing had denied her the chance to travel, so she was delighted when I informed her that I was off to Singapore for a long working holiday.

She gave me three months, which was the usual stay for social visit pass holders. I gave myself three weeks. The eternal optimist. Seven years later, I'm still here and my dear old nan living in east London is still asking her neighbours: "Is it common for people to have seven-year holidays? It never was in my day. We either got a day out at the seaside or we went to the countryside to do a bit of scrumping at the local orchard. Do they have seaside places in Singapore? I still don't know why he wanted to go to China in the first place."

But that's my batty grandmother. Let me give you an idea, if I may, of what a truly unique woman my mother is. Though she rarely says anything positive about me (until I was 15, I thought there was a linguistic rule which stipulated that the words "Neil", "fuck" and "off" always had to go in the same sentence), I know living 10,000 km away is difficult for her. Yet she doesn't want me to leave Singapore, despite never having visited the city-state.

She knows I have economic and personal security and live in a completely safe environment that is now only guaranteed in small pockets of England. Just recently she said on the phone: "I know you could get a decent job here and earn better money, but did I tell you about the bloke who was stabbed down at the harbour last week?... No?... Well, he died on Tuesday." She's full of chirpy vignettes like that.

But I have to concede that my time away from England has given me a greater respect for Singapore's emphasis on filial piety. When I discovered what it meant, I was initially skeptical. Teachers, parents and politicians are constantly being urged to inculcate positive family values in the nation's children. I thought it was a governmental cop-out. We don't have a welfare state or pensions for the citizens who gave us fifty years of their working lives so you'll just have to take care of your own parents or they will starve, seemed to be the government's line of thought. Moreover I still read about greedy children fighting over the estate of their dead parents like incorrigible vultures squabbling over carrion.

Nevertheless, I have Singaporean friends who look after their ageing parents and relatives simply because it is the right thing to do. There's no ulterior motive. And with every act of filial piety I come across, the more aware I become of the distance between my family and myself. My youngest brother was three years old when I left for university and six when I settled in Singapore. Aside from missing most of his childhood, I'm also completely out of sync with his interests and understanding of popular culture. First, it was *Thomas the Tank Engine*, and then it was *Star Wars*. When I last visited, I asked: "So what do you think of Darth Maul then?"

"Shut up you sad twat," he replied, kicking me in the balls and flipping me onto my back like a rag doll. "I'm The Rock."

"You're a rock?"

"No, stupid. I'm The Rock."

"Oh, are you?"

"Yeah. Can you smell what The Rock's cooking?"

"You've learnt how to cook? That's great."

"No, stupid. God, don't you know anything? That's what the wrestler, The Rock, says."

"Does he? That's marvellous, Gary. Do you think you could stop sitting on my head now?"

I missed almost 10 years of that brotherly banter. I also wasn't around when my grandparents died. They passed away within two months of each other. Now, this may sound cold and heartless, but when you live abroad, a certain detachment inevitably results. Distant relatives pass away and you're sad, but the sense of loss can never be the same because they are names spoken over the telephone. You didn't visit them in the hospital. You didn't watch them deteriorate. And you didn't attend their funerals.

To some degree, it was the same with my grandparents. They were in tremendous pain for several months before they died. And of course the illness of one only further exacerbated the suffering of the other. But I never saw any of that. The last time I saw them was at their house, when my grandmother told me I had a deformed neck and looked like the giraffe on the cover of my previous book. I wasn't there for my own mother as she watched her stepfather and then her mother slowly waste away in a hospital bed. I didn't even go to my grandparents' funerals. I offered to come back, but my mother said there really was no point. Remember them how they were, before they got sick, she said. She's right, of course, but her pragmatism did nothing for the guilt I felt when I returned at Christmas and my grandparents were not there anymore. Then it hits you just how detached you've become. Then you realise that not being able to do anything was not an excuse for not coming back. I should've been there with my family.

Fortunately, I had an emotional crutch to lean on, didn't I? Because in Singapore, I am part of a much larger 'family', aren't I? A 'family' that could have appreciated my confused state of detachment and loss, because these guys are all in the same boat as me. There are always my *ang moh* brothers and sisters ready and willing to embrace me in a foreign land, aren't there? Those Singaporean expatriates all ready to muck in together, get pissed together, console each other, recreate their western ways of life together and generally overlook the fact that they are no longer in a western country. Being so far away from their loved ones, it's understandable that they should seek to be part of a bigger 'family' in Singapore. It just shouldn't be predominately white.

When my grandparents were ailing, my mood in the office was, naturally, not the best so a Singaporean colleague tried to cheer me up. "What you worried about?" he said. "Go to that British pub in Boat Quay. Find a few *ang moh*s. Can talk, reminisce about English weather and then go out and bang a few local women. What's the problem?"

Call me naive, but I've never done that in my life. I was never good-looking enough for a start. But in Singapore, there are plenty who have. They really are one big happy family in an Asian land. You've met them, right? In the various jobs that I've had here, I've had the pleasure of meeting dozens of my so-called fellow family members. Some have a resume that's so shady, you'll need a torchlight to read its 15 pages. They've either been a principal at some obscure language school in Made-up Street, Swansea, Wales, where the register contained four students, two sheep and a shepherd called Taffy Williams, who'd only ever conversed with four-legged mammals. Or you get the journalist who was night editor at the *Liechtenstein Times* and has written award-winning columns, apparently, for the *Cockroach Collectors Journal* and the *Sheep Dip Recipe Guide* (old Taffy Williams was a subscriber).

One of my favourite Singaporean *ang moh*s, though, is the 'foreign, talented' footballer. In my line of work, I've met quite a few. This guy has played for every English club you've never heard of and claims to be better than David Beckham was when they played in the England Under-Fives together. He could "have been a contender, Charlie", but Beckham stole his apple juice after the match, so they had a fight, he lost and the psychological scar has blighted his playing career ever since. Will Singapore reach the World Cup finals in 2010 by bringing in such stars to enhance the local football scene? Singapore couldn't reach a community cup final in Woodlands with these con artists. I've watched local footballers listen politely while these English professionals (oh, they're pros alright) discuss their knowledge and all the time I know the Malay lads are thinking: "If you're that good, why the fuck would you come to Singapore to play for $5,000 a month and deprive one of us of a first-team place?" The answer is, of course, so that the overweight beer barrel can join up with his happy *ang moh* gang here and live like a 19th century colonial.

In all fairness, Singaporeans could think the same of me. It's a natural assumption to make. But unlike other *ang moh*s I've encountered, I didn't come here because I couldn't find work anywhere else. Being 21, I'd never worked anywhere else. Aside from six months in a London stockbrokers' office, I came here seven years ago with nothing but some decent qualifications, a Game Boy, bags of enthusiasm and a rather dwarfish, but brilliant architect called Scott. I've worked my balls off ever since. It's always been an honest, two-way relationship and I sleep soundly at night. Some of these 'talented', 'experienced' *ang moh*s must require huge condos to fit all their skeletons into their closets. If I meet one more suspect teacher, footballer or businessman, who thinks he's Mr. Chips, Michael Owen or Richard Branson, I'm calling Singapore Immigration. You should too.

In some ways, though, you can't blame these deceivers. Utilising their capacity for extreme bullshit, they're capitalising on the white-man bias to enjoy the kind of respectable living their mediocre skills really don't deserve. It's up to those Singaporean bananas, and we all know a banana or two, to wheedle out these buggers and drive them from the country. 'Foreign' really isn't a guarantee of 'talent'. Sometimes, it can mean 'a complete fucking waste of space'. Well, it does in my dictionary.

Ironically, these *ang moh*s will force me to leave this country quicker than any Singaporean. Their hypocrisy is nauseating. I don't want to be tarred with the same brush. Keep me well away from that 'family', please. At times, I've found myself cornered by one or two at a pub or some social function. Not often, but it happens. The bullshit goes into overdrive. I hear about this 'deal' and that 'deal', this 'contact' and that 'contact' and how cheap it is to have a maid in this country. And I laugh. Their cover would be blown in seconds in a place like Dagenham and they know it. With all that verbal diarrhoea, the residents of my old hometown would smell them coming a mile off. That's why these wankers will never leave Singapore, not while they can still smooth talk their way into a luxurious lifestyle. They will never return to their actual family in the west. They're having too much fun with their adopted family in the east.

But I will. Undoubtedly, Singapore's been nothing but good to me. However, those family ties, both in England and Australia, have been stretched to the limit. Sooner rather than later, I will be surrounded with predominantly white people again. The major difference being my parents don't live in condos they don't deserve, nor do they profess to having enough skills and working experience to justify a five-page resume. Instead, we'll sit around and laugh as my mother tells stories about half-naked nurses. Surreal, perhaps, but honest. And that suits me fine. After seven years in Singapore, I've heard enough *ang moh* bullshit to last a lifetime.

THE LOVERS

WATCHING your grandparents going through the preliminary stages of sexual foreplay is something you tend not to forget. When she was barely five years old, my mother decided to hide under the kitchen table while her 70-year-old grandmother did the washing up. For reasons she never did divulge, the old matriarch often favoured a baggy string vest with no bra on while she did the dishes.

On this particular occasion, her husband came in and sneaked up behind her, grabbing a part of her body that had long since given up the fight against gravity. Then, he kindly said: "Ooh, You've still got a fine pair of knockers there, haven't you, love?" The elderly pair both giggled. He went back and read the paper, she finished the washing up and my stunned mother vowed never to play hide-and-seek on her own again.

Outraged members of the moral brigade, who tend not to get out enough, would denounce such a vulgar incident. But, it's a wonderful story.

My great-grandparents endured tremendous hardship in a post-war London. They lived in the east London borough of Bethnal Green, which was ravaged by the Blitz and largely ignored by Westminster policymakers. Yet they loved each other dearly. And they went at it like rabbits until my great-granddad died. A heart attack killed him. I'm not bloody surprised. My great-grandmother lived on for another 20 years and died a week before her 90th birthday. But she never did the washing up with the same vigour after her husband died.

But I was truly delighted to discover that my great-grandparents were not alone. In late March 2002, some 300 Singaporeans, many of them elderly, picked up and passed on love tips at a public forum. That's right. A load of oldies voluntarily came together to discuss their relationships. From keeping the partner happy in the bedroom to learning to duck when the wife attempts decapitation with a kitchen plate, many aspects of maintaining a harmonious marriage were discussed.

This forum, which was organised by the Singapore Action Group of Elders and *Lianhe Zaobao*, has unearthed 300 Singaporean superheroes. There were men in their 80s asking, quite sincerely, how they could sustain their sex lives. Aware of my 'energy levels', I'll be lucky if I can raise a smile when I'm 80, never mind anything else. I'm fairly sure that the word "erection" will not be part of my vocabulary by then. Words like "adult", "diapers" and "incontinence" almost certainly, but not "erection".

My favourite hero at the forum was a hip 86-year-old, clad in jeans and sunglasses, who wanted to know how he could be more loving to his wife. How he could be more loving? What a truly humbling thought. Apparently, there was another elderly chap suffering from a failing sex drive and seeking views on how it could be rectified. He asked: "My wife is demanding and I'm not getting any younger, you know. I'm worried I can no longer satisfy her. We used to make love every day but now, it's dropped to six times a week. What should I do?"

The virility of some of these old-timers is terrifying. I'm only 28 and, increasingly, my idea of a night of hedonistic pleasure is a DVD and a bowl of instant noodles. Yet, there are couples who were making babies long before the People's Action Party was born and they're still doing the business in the bedroom.

At the time of the forum, Singapore was enveloped in a gloomy depression, thanks to the war in the Middle East and the deadly virus at its doorstep. But the trusty elderly led the way once more, by coming together to discuss the importance of a loving marriage. I just wish the nation's pioneers could hang around for another 50 years to sort out the younger generations. Though, I've heard rumours that if anything does go wrong, one or two of the more prominent senior citizens will rise from their graves to correct any problems. I certainly hope so. They speak about love and relationships, while their dour children fret over the economy, incompetent maids and the latest ringtones. Where did it all go wrong?

We needed these fun-loving pensioners at the recent Rolling Stones' gig. Some friends of mine managed to secure a couple of tickets by forfeiting most of their CPF savings and were rewarded with some good seats, which they found once they'd fought past the middle-aged Caucasian men with young Singaporean women that made up much of the audience, of course.

During the concert, my friends received a public dressing down — for having the audacity to sing along to the Stones' classic *Angie*. Fancy that! Singing at a rock concert! What a gaggle of selfish, inconsiderate bastards! Quick, grab the cane and bring back public flogging before this self-destructive nation descends into anarchy.

In fairness, I've heard my friends sing before. Collectively, they sound like a goose farting in the fog. But, that's hardly a cause for complaint, is it? It was for a group of women, in their early 30s, who were sitting in front. One of them turned and said: "We must thank you, gentlemen, for ruining a beautiful song." To which my friend replied: "You're most welcome. I usually charge for our performances, but seeing as you are devoid of a sense of fun, a personality and, quite possibly, a life, you may continue to listen to us geese — free of charge. You miserable fuckers."

My Singaporean superheroes wouldn't have tolerated such sullen behaviour. "Now listen here, young lady," one of the 80-year-olds would've retorted. "You think you've got problems. You youngsters moan about the economy, the price of cars and HDB flats. Well, listen to me missy. I'm 82 years old and now, I can only get it up six times a week. So, get some perspective and get down to *Jumping Jack Flash*."

Let's hire these virulent, vivacious aunties and uncles to track down boring buggers islandwide. They've been around long enough to know what it's all about. After all, they talk 'love' while everyone else talks 'war'. Sounds bloody good to me.

THE HUNCHBACK

SHORT of chopping my head off and handing it to the bus driver, I don't know what else to do on single-deck buses. For the umpteenth time, I suffered a right bloody whack against the roof of the bus as the excitable driver treated his handbrake like a bicycle pump. Fellow commuters were treated to an *ang moh* beanpole rubbing his head furiously and shouting: "I've hit my fucking head... again."

In some respects, my lack of courtesy to my fellow passengers can be attributed to the Singapore Science Centre. Don't get me wrong, I love the place and I believe every child should visit it at least once a year. When I was in primary school in England, we took annual coach trips to London's Science Museum. The excursions were so tedious that the highlight was the peanut butter sandwiches on the bus, largely because they weren't mine to start with. I had cheese. But my old mate, Ross, used to decorate the windows with his cornflakes just as we pulled out of Dagenham. So the tear-stained teacher got her handkerchief ruined, and I got Ross' peanut butter sandwiches. There was very little educational advancement involved during these museum trips.

I suspect that's why I get a tad irritated at the impressive Singapore Science Centre. Its hands-on exhibits merely serve to remind me that I have the scientific understanding of plankton. My mathematical knowledge barely gets me through a *Barney* VCD with my Singaporean goddaughter. Now Nicole's moved on to *Sesame Street*, I struggle to keep up with Bert and Ernie's number counting. Incidentally, are those two gay? Only I've never seen them in the company of women, have you? And they're always bloody smiling.

Back in the Science Centre, I was attempting, unsuccessfully, to take a number of wooden bricks of various shapes and sizes and fit them into a cohesive cube. A 10-year-old boy, patiently waiting for his turn behind me, whispered words of encouragement like: "*ang moh* so stupid" and "so slow, blur like *sotong* (squid)" just to spur me along.

Finally, his patience snapped: "*Aiyoh* can I show you how? ... Okay, this rectangle goes there, you see? ... That square one fits in there and you turn that round ... *aiyoh* ... you had that one upside down ... *wah lau* ... and then you slot that one inside the hole and you're finished, can?"

"Look, I went to university, you know?" I hissed, in a rather pathetic effort to resurrect my self-esteem. The brat's brief, but vocal, demonstration, had drawn a crowd.

"University ... Really ah? ... *Wah lau* ... Can I take it apart and build it for myself now?"

"Of course. Tell me, have you ever put the cube together after being poked in the eye?"

"No."

"Well, now's your chance. You little bastard."

We left the Science Centre soon after. Apart from the cube

incident, the security guard caught me going down the slide in the pre-school playground. Shouting "whoopee" was probably not a good idea.

An hour later, I was performing my excruciating, cabaret routine for a captive audience on my local SBS Transit bus. The No. 232 is a single-deck feeder bus that serves the residents of Toa Payoh Lorong 2. And when I board, young children actually cry: "Mummy, here comes the *Homo erectus* man. He's so funny. He can clean the roof with his neck and sweep the floor of the bus with his knuckles ... all at the same time!"

You see, I am 1.92 metres tall. And single-deck buses in Singapore aren't. Scraping my neck and shoulders along the roof of the miniature buses, I have collected everything from bus tickets to stunned mosquitoes saying to each other, "what the fuck was that?" in my collar.

On that brief journey following my sojourn to the Science Centre, I suffered multiple neck lesions and stumbled around the packed No. 232 bus like Frankenstein's monster. By the end of the trip, I had perfected the posture of Quasimodo and staggered off the bus a full two inches shorter than when I had boarded, shouting: 'The bells! The bells! They make me deaf, you know?"

Unsurprisingly, I wholeheartedly concur with a couple of Singaporeans, who recently asked SBS Transit for more double-deck bus services. The transport authority replied that on certain bus routes that just isn't feasible, due to a number of tree-lined avenues and low flyovers.

What kind of excuse is that? Has no one at SBS Transit seen James Bond's *Live and Let Die*? In one scene, the fleeing Roger Moore steals a bus and coolly drives it through a tunnel, slicing it in half, without raising even one of his trademark eyebrows.

Now that could work. It would certainly reduce stuffiness on the upper deck and create more headroom for those who remembered to duck. But I doubt the transport authorities would approve. An SBS Transit spokesman would soon be informing the general public: "We'd like to reassure passengers and remind drivers that removing the top half of their buses is not permitted, even on humid days. Whether it is via a tunnel, a bridge or any low-lying apparatus for that matter, unapproved bus separations would litter the roads, disrupt traffic flow and scratch the buses' expensive paintwork. And we've only just changed the logos on most buses, so that could prove rather troublesome.

"But we thank Quasimodo for his feedback and suggest a weekly massage to reduce the hump."

So, in desperation, I'm turning to the guillotine. That's the only solution for lanky buggers like me on single-deck buses. Place a sensor-triggered guillotine above the ez-link card reader. Anyone who registers above 1.9 metres in height gets his head lopped off. That'll speed up commuter flow and increase headroom, so I'm sure the transport authorities will commission a guillotine feasibility study.

Apparently, Joseph Ignace Guillotin, who championed the cause of painless executions during the French Revolution, was most unhappy at having his name attached to such a murderous device. He only advocated more humane killings, not the actual machine that had been around for centuries. Until his death, he sought to distance himself from the old head-chopper. Both in literature and literally I would have thought. But then, old Guillotin never travelled around Toa Payoh in single-deck buses, did he? I do, every hump-inducing day. So get that bloody blade sharpened.

THE PROTECTORS

UNDERSTANDABLY, many concerned Singaporean parents have been obsessed with their children's personal protection and cleanliness of late. My mother was no different. She, too, was preoccupied with my personal hygiene, or complete lack of, when I was growing up in England. She would challenge my powers of contortion by making impossible requests, such as: "Just look at the dirt behind your ear, you dirty bastard."

Invariably, I would cut my head in half and examine the aforementioned area. Her frequent threats of death were most unnerving. On hearing that I'd crossed the road without checking both sides first, she'd bellow: "How many times do I have to tell you? I mean it, Neil. If you get run over by a bus, I'll bloody kill you!"

My personal favourite, though, was when she spotted a smudge on my face on the way home from school. Employing a technique popular with many British mothers, she'd take out a tissue, spit on it, or in some cases lick it, and then, scrub my face with it. Having rubbed a hole into my cheek, she would stand back, admire her handiwork and say: "There, that's better."

"What do you mean, 'that's better'? I've got a face full of your saliva and a smidgeon of lipstick and I've lost all feeling in my cheek." I usually got a slap on the other cheek for that. It helped to balance the redness on both sides.

With the spread of a deadly virus, Singaporeans have been concerned with the hygiene standards of their children and their families recently and it's a legitimate concern. There have been rational requests to don face masks in crowded areas, wear gloves when handling food or rubbish and use tissues when sneezing. But the need for greater personal protection becomes a tad irritating when it descends into moralising, not to mention patronising, condemnation.

I've lost count of the number of letters written to the media that have said: "Please don't spit, ladies and gentlemen, in the street, at each other, or on your own clothes, because spitting is ... wait for it ... bad."

At this point, I assume four million Singaporeans are supposed to jump up simultaneously and cry: "That's it! My god, she's bloody right, you know? Spitting is bad. Give that woman a hankie."

Perhaps we should rename Singapore 'Asia's Animal Farm' and we can all wear woolly jumpers, crawl around on all fours and bleat: "Spitting bad, hankies good. Spitting bad, hankies good".

This condescending fluff reminds me of a letter I received recently from an irate reader who criticised me for making fun of that poor, much maligned dictator Saddam Hussein. She challenged me on this and felt the need to point out that — now get ready for this — "War costs lives".

Do you ever wonder who these Singaporeans are? I do. They must pore over the newspapers every day, shouting: "Filth!

Outrageous! Smut! How dare he try to be funny in this deadly serious world we live in? Filth! He's left me with no choice. I must point out that war costs lives. He can't possibly know that. And then, when I'm through with that insensitive cretin, I'm going to remind all Singaporeans that spitting is just, well, bad. Filth! Baa."

Of course, I can't deny that there are still some pockets of resistance among the saliva gang in Singapore. There are some spitting gold medal contenders in my Toa Payoh estate, but then there are Dagenham teenagers who smash beer bottles in the High Street of my own hometown when they're pissed. These parasites do exist. It doesn't mean we should waste oxygen or ink advising others not to follow suit.

Yet, the National Environment Agency obviously disagrees. As I write this, I'm looking at a marvellous advisory that the Agency published in a newspaper recently. The letter reminded Singaporeans that it is an offence to "spit or expel mucous". I didn't even know what "expel mucous" meant. I thought it was the stage name of a nightclub DJ, as in "Fat Boy Slim and Expel Mucous". That could work.

My own regret was that the letter wasn't longer, otherwise I would have framed it and hung it in the living room. But at least, it saved the best for last. The last sentence included the suggestion that "those who find that they have to spit or blow their nose should do so with a piece of tissue paper". Because you weren't sure, were you? But if the Agency is capable of giving out such sound advice, it shouldn't stop there. The advisory could have continued: "We'd also like to remind Singaporeans that walking can be achieved by putting one foot in front of the other. Where possible, try to perform the act in a straight line to avoid bumping into your fellow walkers. Thus considerably reducing the chances of you spitting in their faces."

The theme of self-protection is everywhere. Fortunately, not all of it is gloomy. My news editor recently handed me a press release and said: "This one's for you, pervert."

Indeed it was. The press release was proud to announce that a reputable condom manufacturer had introduced a bigger condom to cater to the well-endowed man.

At a time when cynical, ruthless companies are exploiting the nation's fears by promoting everything from hand cream to anti-bacterial toilet paper, the big condom campaign stands out as the work of a marketing genius. The new, enlarged product is supposed to be 2 mm thicker than existing condoms. But whether or not you actually need the extra space is utterly irrelevant, isn't it? Men will be queuing up in supermarkets and convenience stores to ask, in very loud voices: "Excuse me. Do you happen to have the new condom that caters for the well-endowed? You know, the one for men who are hung like horses?"

Apparently, the condom company held in-house tests and 97% of users preferred the bigger product. How were these tests conducted? More importantly, how does one participate?

The National Environment Agency has emphasised the importance of improving one's personal protection in Singapore. So I am more than willing to take part in the next in-house condom test. In times of trouble, I must be prepared to go the extra 2 mm for the nation.

THE CHARACTERS

AMONG my family and friends, I was fortunate enough to be surrounded by a number of imbalanced individuals while I was growing up in England. Spending time with some serious cuckoos builds character, according to my mother. But then, I think she just used that as an excuse. When she was sweeping the kitchen floor once, she suddenly had a schizophrenic seizure and thought she was legendary batter Babe Ruth. At least, I think that's why she chased me around the living room, trying to hit my head with the broom handle for a home run. But, rather deftly, I deflected the blow with my right ear and she only made first base.

But dealing with slightly left-of-centre characters became a regular occurrence during my childhood. On the corner of my street was Maltese Tony. A wonderfully considerate and kind bloke who had emigrated from Malta to Dagenham when he was a young man. If you've ever seen both the stunning landscapes of Malta and the council housing estates of Dagenham, you would immediately gain a basic understanding of Maltese Tony. He had screws loose.

On arriving, it seems that the first English expression he heard was "mind you", but he never fully grasped its meaning, so he never said it in context. He said things like, "I have to go to the mind you shop to buy some cigarettes." The fact that he also had an incurable stutter never helped matters. I'm not making this up. When he stuttered, he became the only human being to experience rapid eye movement while he was awake. Blinking furiously, he would say: "I was stuck in a bastard m-m-m-mind you traffic jam for 20 m-m-m-mind you minutes yesterday." To make matters worse, he was a taxi driver. And taxi drivers were expected to engage in a little small talk. The only problem was his small talk could take an hour.

But his *piéce de résistance* was his complete lack of awareness behind a steering wheel. The world never existed when he was driving the car. The fact that he was a taxi driver only made it all the more fun, or terrifying if you were the passenger. His favourite trick was the 'homemade cigarette'. Stopping at a traffic light, he would pull out his tobacco tin, take out a pinch of tobacco, spread it out across a small, square piece of cigarette paper and then carefully roll it into a cigarette. Making these nicotine-filled burritos used to be quite popular in Britain. But the process was time-consuming. It could take up to five minutes. He would do it at a busy road junction, where the traffic lights changed every 30 seconds. And, frankly speaking, he didn't give a shit. Frustrated car drivers would scream abuse, bang on their horns and screech around him and he'd be completely oblivious. Eventually he would get annoyed and shout: "Why are you making all this bastard mind you n-n-n-noise? You bastards."

He was fond of the word 'bastard'. If he still hadn't finished and the complaints around him intensified, he would really lose it. "I can't even make a m-m-m mind you bastard cigarette in peace, without you making all this n-n-n-noise. You mind you bastards!"

"Er, excuse me," his startled passenger would finally pipe up. "I think they are shouting at you. The traffic lights keep changing and you still haven't moved."

"Who was mind you talking to you? This is none of your business. Get out of my taxi, you mind you bastard!" He would throw so-called mind you dangerous passengers out of his vehicle every week and then complain that the job paid meagre wages.

To be honest, I thought I'd never be fortunate enough to meet anyone as quirky as Maltese Tony again. In England, he's one in a million. But in Toa Payoh, he'd just be one of the residents living in my estate. There was a fine collection of entertainers in my old block in Lorong 1 and, having moved in recent months to Lorong 2, I miss them dearly. My favourite was Rock DJ Auntie. In truth, she was once the infamous 'bra lady', whom I've mentioned before. But in the last year or so, the mad old bat went through a stunning metamorphosis that would've made Kafka proud.

'Bra lady' was famous, in my old HDB block at least, for travelling up and down in lifts all day, stopping at every floor. She performed this civic duty while wearing a pink bra on the OUTSIDE of her clothes. The cups were so large, they wouldn't have looked out of place on an ageing elephant. But, alas, that's all in the past. Now, she's Rock DJ auntie. My girlfriend reported the transformation one evening. Out of breath, she ran into the flat and said: "I've just seen bra lady coming back from the shops!"

"So what? We see her nearly every day. Pink bloody bra and everything."

"No, but she's not wearing the bra today."

"Well, you don't expect her to wear it every day, do you? I'm sure even she must take it off occasionally, otherwise the stench would knock her out."

"Shut up and come and see. She's wearing something else."

And she most certainly was. When I was growing up in the late '70s, my parents had a pair of those, enormous leather-padded headphones to plug into the hi-fi. Do you remember them? They had a plug the size of a screwdriver and when you put them on you looked like Princess Leia in *Star Wars*. Well, old 'bra lady' was wearing the biggest pair of those old leather-padded headphones that I'd ever seen. Think Princess Leia some 30 years after menopause and you'll get a rough picture of what I saw across the void deck. 'Bra lady' was dead. Long live Rock DJ Auntie.

Transfixed, we sat at one of those concrete tables that really make your bum itch and watched her approach. Then came the revelation. The giant headphones were plugged in — to nothing. The coiled lead was hanging loosely by the side of her body. Quite clearly, I could see the screwdriver plug brushing against her knee. What the hell was the purpose of those headphones? Earmuffs? In Singapore? This woman was utterly insane.

Or perhaps she is a genius. Just two days before writing this, I saw her again. Whenever I smile at her, she never reciprocates, her vacant, slightly puzzled expression never changes. Rock DJ Auntie looks right through me as if I'm transparent. Then it occurred to me, perhaps I am. She is on another dimension to the rest of us, mentally speaking. She has reached another level and is communicating on a higher spiritual plane. The signs were always there, weren't they? Of course, she doesn't need to plug her headphones into any electrical source because her power source is looking down at us and not the other way around. That's what the pink bra was – a signal no less. A polyester satellite communicating earthly messages to an outerworldly paymaster. Yes, that's the answer. Everything is clear now.

On the other hand, of course, she could be a complete fucking lunatic.

It would be grossly unfair, however, to categorise Madam Bed Linen as a lunatic. Slightly off kilter perhaps, but she's so endearing, she's almost edible. Short and rather plump, she doesn't quite reach to my chest which makes our brief liaisons all the more memorable. About six months ago, we were in Toa Payoh Central hunting for a new quilt, bedsheets, pillowcases and so on. As a rule, I find this kind of shopping about as entertaining as plugging into headphones without a Walkman. But as I tend to emit the odd comical sound while I'm in bed, I was forced to concede that I was partially responsible for the demise of the old quilt.

Luckily, Madam Bed Linen introduced herself and I've since bought three quilt cover sets. We were in a small department store, one of those that always sticks an employee in the bed linen section, assuming perhaps that if we have a blue-and-yellow bedroom, we would need those colours pointed out to us by a conscientious shop assistant. We can't take the bedroom with us, right? So it's better to be safe than sorry. Normally, I have little patience with these shop assistants. I know they are only doing their job, but I get irritated when you tell them your bedroom is indeed blue and yellow and they show you the remains of an explosion in a paint factory and tell you that it will match.

But Madam Bed Linen in Toa Payoh was different. Firstly, she never stopped giggling and mumbling to herself, which was a little disconcerting initially. She also spoke in a high-pitched voice and agreed with everything you said. We'd say: "We actually want a blue-and-yellow set."

"Ha! Blue and yellow. This one okay?"

"It's pink."

"Yeah, very nice."

"We want blue-and-yellow."

"Ha! You want blue-and-yellow... How about this one?"

"It's a plain, white quilt."

"Yeah, it's a plain quilt. But it's cheap, got offer one."

"But we want a blue-and-yellow one."

"Ha ha! You want a blue-and-yellow one?"

It began to feel like a Jedi mind trick after a while. But the best thing about Madame Bed Linen was actually two-fold. Firstly, she had a slight lisp. And secondly, she pronounced sheet as 'seat'. After we'd selected a quilt, she asked: "Beth-seat for you, sir?"

"I'm sorry?"

"Ha ha, would you like some beth-seats?" She pointed at the bedsheets and I had to walk away, complaining of a throat irritation. I know this is terrible, and I'm going straight to hell, but I bit my tongue, returned to this lovely lady and formulated as many ways as possible to make her say "bed-sheets". Picking up a quilt cover, I would say: "Would these fit on a queen-sized bed?"

"Ha ha! That's a quilt cover, not beth-seats."

"What are these blue ones?"

"Ah, they are okay. They're beth-seats."

Now, whenever she spots me in the store, she shouts cheerfully: "Hello, ha ha! Beth-seats, I got beth-seats. You wanna see my beth-seats? Ha ha!" Her inexhaustible chirpiness whenever we meet attracts some concerned stares.

Every time she invites me to see her bedsheets, she sounds like a middle-aged hooker with a speech impediment. But she's wonderful company and I always have a chat with her when I'm in the shop, no matter what I'm doing. She never says she's too busy and will make time to talk, like the majority of the Singaporeans I meet in and around Toa Payoh. When I was promoting my previous book, a journalist said he'd lived in Singapore all his life and had never encountered half the characters that I claim to have met in a small corner of Toa Payoh. He suggested it was due to the novelty factor. A white man in Toa Payoh evokes reaction and curiosity. People are generally nosy by nature and will seek to find out what the *ang moh* is doing in their lift, void deck or coffee shop. It's a possibility, though a touch patronising. Neighbours and strangers are naturally inquisitive, it's hardly a crime. And call me self-indulgent, but I will actively go out of my way to meet people in my estate and chat with them. That was the reason I decided to travel in the first place.

Life is so fast-paced now, apparently, that there is no time for small talk. You know, a little bit of harmless nonsense that helps break up the mundane and makes a predictable working day more fun. When interested Singaporeans take a *kaypoh* interest in my life, I respond. It's not exactly profound. I don't give a two-word answer and disappear into a lift, like many of the younger executive types do in my block. These hardworking chaps may not be unhinged, quirky or colourful. They're just boring.

Observe the HDB void decks. Invariably, they are filled with old-timers doing nothing except gossip and chat. Occasionally, they have the odd beer to lubricate the old vocal cords. Among the younger generation, conversation (at least conversation that doesn't involve the economy, gambling or golf) is a dying art in Singapore. It's no coincidence that most of my favourite eccentrics are amomng the elderly. They like to talk and I like to listen. It's not a complex relationship.

Similarly, Singaporean children can't seem to keep their mouths shut either. It's fabulous. Not yet tainted by race, religion or politics, they rarely hold back. There's a gang of primary school kids from my old block who are a sublime mix of innocence, honesty and insanity. Indeed, the cheeky bastards are so open and gregarious that they could have had me arrested.

For a couple of years now, they've been playing football on the void deck. That's how I met them. A mixture of Chinese and Malay boys aged from six to around 12, they're more streetwise than Jack Dawkins and audaciously insist the "tall *ang moh* come play" every time I pass. Our ad hoc five-a-side matches had attracted some curious glances. But that was nothing compared to the reactions I get from strangers now, whenever the boys shout their greetings.

Almost two years ago, a journalist came to my flat with a photographer to interview me about my first book, *Notes from an even Smaller Island*. We took some photos in front of the block while my football posse playfully mocked me in the background. The interviewer suggested taking some pictures with my 'gang', but they refused. Normally, you can't get the boys to shut up. On this occasion, though, they were struck dumb by stage fright. Fair enough.

However, once the journalist and the photographer had left, the gang's cockiness quickly returned. About a week after the interview, I was walking home with the missus when the gang waved at me from the children's playground. One of them shouted: "Hello, *ang moh*. You remember us, you wanted to take our photograph last time? Do you remember? You wanted to take our photograph!" At that moment, if I'd produced an axe and screamed "Here's Johnny!", I don't think my girlfriend could have expressed greater horror. I tried to explain the boy's claim.

"No, it wasn't me who wanted to take your photograph was it, boys?"

"Yeah lah, it was you what," replied the cheeky one. "You wanted to take photographs of all of us, with you also in the photograph, right?" I could have strangled the little bastard.

But it never stopped. To this day, if I bump into any of the young void deck footballers, they bellow: "Hello, remember us? You wanted to take photographs of us? You want to take now?" And they always say it just as a respectable, middle-aged couple is crossing my path. Their timing is impeccable. My girlfriend is constantly on hand to remind me that I have the unsmiling face of a serial killer, so the kids' banter is just enough to have people crossing the road to avoid me.

They surpassed themselves, however, when my girlfriend's parents came to Singapore for her graduation ceremony. Arriving back at the block after a day of sightseeing, we were discussing our evening plans when the void deck boys spotted me.

"Hello *ang moh*. Remember me?"

"Yes, I remember you. How can I forget you? You're here every day."

"Yeah lah. You remember you wanted to take our photograph last time. You want to take it now?" The boys giggled. My future parents-in-law questioned their daughter's judgment.

"Look, for the last time. I never asked to take your picture."

"Don't bluff ah. You always ask to take our photograph what?" More giggling.

"No I don't."

"Okay lah, never mind. Next time can ... You want to play with our balls instead?"

Well, the dropping pin was deafening. And before you say anything, they were referring to their bloody footballs! They always took more than one because the surplus balls were used as goal posts opposite the void deck pillars. Both my girlfriend and I spent half the night explaining this to her parents, while retelling the journalist/photographer story. Though I've been forced to concede since that the possibility of carrying a camera with me, on the off chance that I should meet the void deck posse, is looking increasingly likely. I could whack the little bastards with it.

They just can't keep their mouths shut, which is unlike my old mini-mart owner who rarely said anything. Except on weekends, when we held the same conversation on every occasion. Handing over my change at the counter, he would smirk and say: "I read your funny column in the newspaper today."

"Yeah?"

"Yeah ... hmm."

And that's all he ever said. He would grin at me, all-knowingly, and hum. It's happened dozens of times. He never comments on the column, never refers to it or makes any further conversation whatsoever. I ask my girlfriend to go in on weekends now, because I know I lack self-restraint.

Recently, he said: "I read your column again ... hmm." And I could feel myself saying: "Hmm fucking what?"

If that wasn't enough, I have a similar chat with a real Toa Payoh lunatic every Saturday. Without fail, she will approach me, usually around lunchtime, and say: "I read your humour column today mate."

"Yeah?"

"Yeah ... it was shit."

But I have no choice but to exercise self-restraint with that fruitcake. I live with her.

Having switched apartments, I no longer come across the living legends of Lorong 1. Aside from 'bra lady'/Rock DJ Auntie, there was Vidal Sassoon, whom I've referred to before. An elderly lady who lost her marbles in 1962, she used to wander around my block and peer into my apartment whenever the mood took her. The poor woman dressed in dirty, ripped clothes, but had the most immaculate hairdo I've ever seen this side of the Oscar's ceremony. But, sadly, I haven't seen her in a year now. She might have died, but I suspect it's more likely that staff at the local mental hospital got fed up with chasing her around Toa Payoh with a big net. Wherever Vidal is right now, I'm sure there isn't a hair out of place.

Now I'm in Lorong 2, I've yet to meet my fellow funny farmers. But I'm not unduly concerned. They usually find me. But there is a postscript to my humming mini-mart owner. Two months after I moved, he sent an email to my office. I'd never even given him the email address. In the email, he said: "I've noticed that you no longer come to my shop so I assume you moved to a new flat. Consequently, our sale of fizzy drinks, particularly the raspberry flavoured one, has dropped significantly. Would you therefore like me to arrange a case of raspberry drink to be delivered to your new apartment? Your shopkeeper." It was a wonderful, piss-taking letter. Though I was disappointed that it didn't contain a single hum.

I love these people. Despite the persistent stereotyping, they're willing to laugh at themselves and God knows, they have absolutely no problem laughing at me. That's why I've never lived anywhere else, but Toa Payoh. Why should I leave? Where would I go? To a condo? I can't see myself spending weekends by a swimming pool, listening to Caucasian con artists spout bullshit all day. Those places are more suited to the clientele at the Cricket and Polo Clubs, where I suspect I'd be about as welcome as a fart on an MRT train.

For the most part, Toa Payoh's residents have been nothing but warm and generous to me. To dismiss such kindness by attributing it to the 'white man factor' is insulting. I've lived in this estate for seven years now. Where's the novelty value in that? It's nonsense.

On top of all that benevolence, of course, are the fringe benefits. Here, I get a giggling old woman offering to show me her 'beth-seats', a geriatric Princess Leia impersonator and cheeky school kids waving their balls at me. True, we had the stuttering Maltese Tony in Dagenham, but nothing compares to the characters in my Singaporean neighbourhood.

With family ties to consider, I have no idea where I will be living five years from now. But wherever it is, the place will have a hell of a lot to live up to. Because Toa Payoh, in my humble opinion, is a bloody great place to live in.

ABOUT THE AUTHOR

NEIL Humphreys grew up in the working-class town of Dagenham, Essex. Despite being mugged there, twice, and enduring one of the most dire comprehensive school educations this side of *Oliver Twist*, he was still criticised by some residents for fleeing with his first-class degree. When they discovered the price of alcohol in Singapore, they said he was welcome to the Chinese province.

Having spent several happy years pretending to be an English speech and drama teacher in Singapore, he now spends his working hours pretending to be a journalist and occasional author. His first book — *Notes from an even Smaller Island* — was critically acclaimed in both Singapore and Malaysia and was one of Singapore's best-selling books in 2002. His mother swears she bought no more than half the copies sold.